위아

중학듣기
모의고사 20회

2

In-Depth Lab

'인뎁스 랩'은 전·현직 교·강사들과 국내외에서 활동하는 native speaker들로 구성된 컨텐츠 연구 집단이다. 기반 자료 수집, 원형 개발, 실전 시뮬레이션 및 시장 조사, 연구 개발 등의 과정을 협업하는 공동체이다. 각각의 교육 과정 설계에 따른 단원별 학습 논리를 세운 다음 이를 최적의 장치로 구현하고 단순화하여 학교, 학원의 교육 환경에 가장 적합한 교재를 개발하는 것이 '인뎁스 랩'의 활동 목적이다.

위아 **중학듣기 모의고사** 2

지은이	In-Depth Lab
발행인	조상현
발행처	더디퍼런스

등록번호	제2015-000237호
주소	서울시 마포구 마포대로 127, 304호
문의	02-725-9988
팩스	02-6974-1237
이메일	thedibooks@naver.com
홈페이지	www.thedifference.co.kr

ISBN 979-11-86217-66-5 (53740)

위아

중학듣기
모의고사

In-Depth Lab 지음

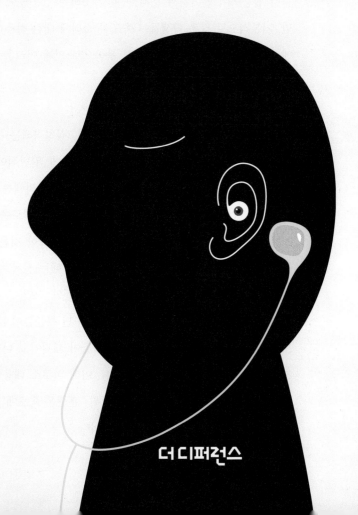

더디퍼런스

머리말 Preface

　　듣기가 안 되는 학생들의 경우에는 한두 개 들리는 단어들을 중심으로 전체 내용 또는 문제의 답을 상상하게 되는데, 말 그대로 상상이기 때문에 정답은 물론 내용에 대한 이해도 어렵다. 나중에 script를 보면서 정답을 맞추다 보면, 모르는 단어가 있었거나, 의미는 알지만 소리로 인식하지 못했거나, 연음되어 개별 단어들이 들리지 않았거나 등등의 여러가지 이유를 발견하게 된다. 그 외에도 잠시 딴 생각을 하느라, 지나간 단어에 집착하느라, 순간 집중력이 떨어져서 문제를 풀지 못하는 경우들도 있을 것이다. 하지만, 기본적으로 많은 학생들이 속도와 소리에 대한 적응, 그리고 듣는 동시에 머리로 내용을 이해하는 훈련 부족으로 인해 어려움을 겪는다고 볼 수 있다.

　　위에서 언급한 속도 적응, 소리 인식, 직청직해는 무엇보다도 반복된 청취를 통해서만 습득될 수 있는 것이기 때문에, 일반적이고 빈번한 주제들에 대해서 무수히 듣고 들을 내용을 확인하는 것 외에는 다른 방도가 없다고 해도 과언이 아닐 것이다. 이를 위해, 계속해서 새로운 청취 지문을 듣고 문제를 푸는 것도 좋은 방법이지만, 이보다 중요한 것은 각각의 지문으로 "완벽 청취" 훈련을 하는 것이다. 한 번 들을 때는 전체 지문에서 몇 가지의 단어만을 catch하게 되지만, 두 번 세 번 듣게 되면, 그 몇 가지의 단어들 주변에 있는 단어들이 들리고 서서히 구멍 난 부분들이 많이 채워지는 것을 느끼게 된다. 이렇게 많은 부분의 단어들이 채워지고 나면 전체 문장 또는 지문의 내용이 메워지는 것을 느끼며, 이때 비로소 내용에 대해 올바른 이해를 할 수 있게 된다. 또한 "완벽 청취" 훈련은 속도에 대한 적응, 소리에 대한 인식, 직청직해 훈련에도 효과적이다.

실질적인 실력 평가를 위해 많은 청취 시험들은 normal speed가 되어가고 있다. Normal이란 우리의 기준이 아닌, 원어민의 기준의 normal로 우리에게는 상당히 빠르게 느껴지는 속도이고, 이런 normal speed가 원어민이 가장 자연스럽게 느끼는 속도라고 했을 때 이에 따라 연음되는 발음들 또한 자연스럽게 많아질 것이다. 그렇기 때문에 더욱 많이 듣고, 익숙해지는 과정이 필요한데, 직청직해는 속도와 소리에 대한 적응 위에 가능할 수 있다.

본 교재는 중학 영어듣기 모의고사를 봐야 하는 학생들을 위한 것이다. 최근 5년간의 기출 문항들을 분석하여 주제나 문제 유형들을 최대한 반영하였고, 점차 길어지고 어려워지는 지문의 길이와 녹음 속도 등을 실정에 맞추었다. 한 번 듣고 문제만 풀고 넘어가는 것이 아니라, 여러 번 듣고 써보는 훈련까지 하기를 당부한다.

역시 왕도는 없다. 반복해서 많이 듣는 것만이 방법이다. 하지만, 얼마나 다행인가? 어떤 특정 사람들만이 할 수 있는 비법이 아니라, 반복해서 많이 듣는 것은 누구나가 할 수 있는 방법이니 말이다.

In-Depth Lab

이 책의 구성

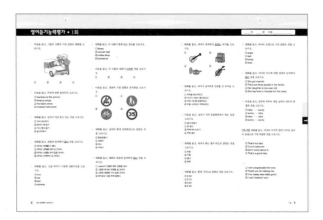

- 모의고사 20회 총 400문제로, 최근까지 출제된 시·도 영어듣기평가 유형들을 포함하여 출제 가능성이 있는 대부분의 유형들을 다루었습니다.

- 학교에서 실시되고 있는 듣기평가와 동일한 구성으로, 한 면에 시험문제가 모두 보이도록 하여 실전에 충실히 대비하게 했습니다.

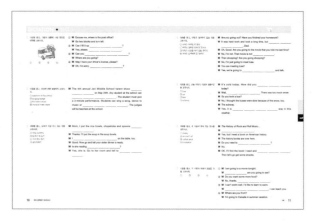

DICTATION

- Tape를 반복하여 들으며, 각 문제의 Script를 훑어보고 중요한 단어 및 표현, 문장을 빈칸에 채워 넣으며 전체 내용을 학습할 수 있습니다.

- 자신의 약점을 파악하여 취약부분을 집중적으로 연습할 수 있습니다.

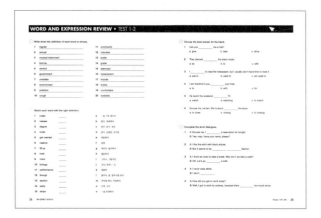

REVIEW

- 지문에서 가장 중요한 어휘를 골라 연습하는 코너입니다.

- 청취 학습의 기본기인 어휘 다지기를 위하여 모의고사 2회분마다 어휘, 숙어를 총정리하여 연습하도록 했습니다. (10회분)

CONTENTS

1 다음을 듣고, 그림의 상황에 가장 알맞은 대화를 고르시오.

①   ②   ③   ④

2 다음을 듣고, 무엇에 관한 설명인지 고르시오.
① teachers at the school
② singing songs
③ the talent show
④ musical instrument

3 대화를 듣고, 남자가 지금 하고 있는 것을 고르시오.
① 저녁 요리하기
② 방에서 책 읽기
③ 식사 준비 돕기
④ 설거지하기

4 대화를 듣고, 내용과 일치하지 <u>않는</u> 것을 고르시오.
① 여자는 숙제를 다 했다.
② 여자는 영화를 보러 갈 것이다.
③ 여자는 쇼핑을 하지 않을 것이다.
④ 여자는 산책하러 갈 것이다.

5 대화를 듣고, 오늘 여자가 이용한 교통수단을 고르시오.
① bus
② car
③ taxi
④ subway

6 대화를 듣고, 두 사람이 현재 있는 장소를 고르시오.
① library
② concert hall
③ coffee shop
④ bookstore

7 다음을 듣고, 두 사람의 대화가 <u>어색한</u> 것을 고르시오.
①   ②   ③   ④

8 다음을 듣고, 내용에 가장 알맞은 표지판을 고르시오.

①   ②

③   ④

9 대화를 듣고, 남자의 현재 장래희망으로 알맞은 것을 고르시오.
① 환경운동가
② 과학자
③ 의사
④ 수의사

10 대화를 듣고, 대화의 내용과 일치하지 <u>않는</u> 것을 고르시오.
① Jason이 선물로 펜과 연필을 샀다.
② 그들은 콘서트 티켓을 살 것이다.
③ 그들은 필통을 사지 않을 것이다.
④ 콘서트는 다음 주에 열린다.

11 대화를 듣고, 여자가 연주하지 <u>못하는</u> 악기를 고르시오.

① ② ③ ④

12 대화를 듣고, 여자가 남자에게 전화를 건 목적을 고르시오.

① 약속을 취소하려고
② 어디가 아픈지 물어보려고
③ 약속 시간을 변경하려고
④ 약을 사오라고 부탁하려고

13 다음을 듣고, 남자가 지역 문화회관에서 하는 일을 고르시오.

① 음식 만들기
② 방 청소
③ 목욕시켜 드리기
④ 주방 청소

14 대화를 듣고, 여자가 하는 말의 의도로 알맞은 것을 고르시오.

① 위로
② 꾸중
③ 충고
④ 축하

15 대화를 듣고, 현재 시각으로 알맞은 것을 고르시오.

① 3:00
② 3:10
③ 3:20
④ 3:30

16 대화를 듣고, 여자의 심경으로 가장 알맞은 것을 고르시오.

① angry
② sad
③ lonely
④ tired

17 대화를 듣고, 여자의 언니에 대한 설명과 일치하지 <u>않는</u> 것을 고르시오.

① She got married.
② There are three people in her family.
③ Her daughter is one year old.
④ She has lived in Canada for five years.

18 다음을 듣고, 남부와 북부의 내일 날씨로 바르게 연결된 것을 고르시오.

① rainy ····· sunny
② sunny ····· rainy
③ rainy ····· rainy
④ sunny ····· sunny

[19~20] 대화를 듣고, 여자의 마지막 말에 이어질 남자의 응답으로 가장 적절한 것을 고르시오.

19

① That's too bad.
② You're welcome.
③ Don't worry about it.
④ That's a good idea.

20

① I will congratulate him now.
② Thank you for helping me.
③ Your essay was really good.
④ I can't believe I won.

1 다음을 듣고, 그림의 상황에 가장 알맞은 대화를 고르시오.

① ② ③ ④

① M Excuse me, where is the post office?

W Go two blocks and turn left.

② M Can I fill it up _____ _____ _____?

W Yes, please. _____ _____ _____.

③ M Can you _____ _____ _____ _____?

W Where are you going?

④ M May I have your driver's license, please?

W Oh, I'm sorry. _____ _____ _____?

2 다음을 듣고, 무엇에 관한 설명인지 고르시오.

① teachers at the school
② singing songs
③ the talent show
④ musical instrument

M The 4th annual Jeil Middle School talent show _____ _____ _____ on May 24th. Any student at the school can _____ _____ _____ _____. The student must give a 3-minute performance. Students can sing a song, dance to music or _____ _____ _____ _____. The judges will be teachers at the school.

3 대화를 듣고, 남자가 지금 하고 있는 것을 고르시오.

① 저녁 요리하기
② 방에서 책 읽기
③ 식사 준비 돕기
④ 설거지하기

M Mom, I put the rice bowls, chopsticks and spoons _____ _____ _____.

W Thanks. I'll put the soup in the soup bowls.

M I _____ _____ _____ _____ on the table, too.

W Good. Now go and tell your sister dinner is ready.

M Is she reading _____ _____ _____?

W Yes, she is. Go to her room and tell to _____ _____ _____.

4 대화를 듣고, 내용과 일치하지 <u>않는</u> 것을 고르시오.

① 여자는 숙제를 다 했다.
② 여자는 영화를 보러 갈 것이다.
③ 여자는 쇼핑을 하지 않을 것이다.
④ 여자는 산책하러 갈 것이다.

M Are you going out? Have you finished your homework?

W It was hard work and took a long time, but _____ _____ _____ _____, Dad.

M Oh, Good. Are you going to the movie that you told me last time?

W No, I'm not. That movie is not _____ _____.

M Then shopping? Are you going shopping?

W No, I'm just going to meet Lisa.

M You are meeting Lisa?

W Yes, we're going to _____ _____ _____ and talk.

5 대화를 듣고, 오늘 여자가 이용한 교통수단을 고르시오.

① bus
② car
③ taxi
④ subway

M It's cold today. How did you _____ _____ _____ today?

W Well, _____ _____ _____. There was too much snow.

M So you took a bus?

W No, I thought the buses were slow because of the snow, too.

M The subway.

W Yes, it is _____ _____ _____ _____ way in this weather.

6 대화를 듣고, 두 사람이 현재 있는 장소를 고르시오.

① library
② concert hall
③ coffee shop
④ bookstore

M *The History of Rock and Roll Music...*

W _____ _____ _____.

M Yes, but I need a book on American history.

W The history books are over here.

M Do you need to _____ _____ _____?

W No.

M OK. I'll find the book I need and _____ _____ _____. Then let's go get some snacks.

7 다음을 듣고, 두 사람의 대화가 <u>어색한</u> 것을 고르시오.

①   ②   ③   ④

① **M** I am going to a movie tonight.
   W _____ _____ are you going to see?

② **M** Do you want some more food?
   W No, thanks. _____ _____ _____.

③ **M** I can't swim well. I'd like to learn to swim.
   W _____ _____ _____ _____, I can teach you.

④ **M** Where are you from?
   W I'm going to Canada in summer vacation.

8 다음을 듣고, 내용에 가장 알맞은 표지판을 고르시오.

① ② ③ ④

M _____ _____! There are too many accidents near schools. Lots of children play or ride bikes near schools. Children are being hurt because cars are going too fast. The government has _____ _____ _____ _____. The speed limit _____ _____ _____ _____ is 30km an hour. Please don't speed.

9 대화를 듣고, 남자의 현재 장래희망으로 알맞은 것을 고르시오.

① 환경운동가
② 과학자
③ 의사
④ 수의사

M _____ _____ _____ the environment.
W The environment?
M Yes, I am worried there is _____ _____ _____.
W Do you want to be a scientist?
M Yes, I do. I will study how pollution hurts animals and humans. So I can help animals and humans _____ _____.
W Good for you.

10 대화를 듣고, 대화의 내용과 일치하지 않는 것을 고르시오.

① Jason이 선물로 펜과 연필을 샀다.
② 그들은 콘서트 티켓을 살 것이다.
③ 그들은 필통을 사지 않을 것이다.
④ 콘서트는 다음 주에 열린다.

M Let's buy Angelia a new pencil case for her birthday.
W Jason _____ _____ _____ for her. He told me.
M Then let's buy _____ _____ _____.
W There must be something better.
M I know. Her favorite group is _____ _____ _____ next week. Let's buy her a ticket.
W Good idea. She will be very happy.

11 대화를 듣고, 여자가 연주하지 <u>못하는</u> 악기를 고르시오.

① (guitar image) ② (piano image)

③ (trumpet image) ④ (cello image)

M Do you play any musical instruments?

W Well, I used to play the piano in an orchestra.

M _____ _____ . Is there any other instrument you can play?

W I'm not a great guitar player, but I know how to play some songs.

M Well, I really want to learn _____ _____ _____ _____ . And I was thinking about learning the trumpet.

W I think the trumpet is hard to learn. Why don't you _____ _____ _____ ?

M You think so?

W Yeah, I can teach you _____ _____ _____ if you want.

---

12 대화를 듣고, 여자가 남자에게 전화를 건 목적을 고르시오.

① 약속을 취소하려고
② 어디가 아픈지 물어보려고
③ 약속 시간을 변경하려고
④ 약을 사오라고 부탁하려고

[Telephone rings.]

M Hello.

W Hi, John. It's Betty. *[cough]*

M Oh, are you sick, Betty?

W Yes, I am.

M So _____ _____ _____ _____ tonight.

W That's right. _____ _____ _____ I am calling.

M Oh, that's too bad. Did you take some medicine? _____ _____ _____ . I hope you feel better soon.

---

13 다음을 듣고, 남자가 지역 문화회관에서 하는 일을 고르시오.

① 음식 만들기
② 방 청소
③ 목욕시켜 드리기
④ 주방 청소

M I want to _____ _____ _____ _____ in my community. _____ _____ _____ at the community center on Saturday afternoons. I don't work in the kitchen. I help the old people _____ _____ _____ . They are not strong, so they need some help cleaning their place.

---

14 대화를 듣고, 여자가 하는 말의 의도로 알맞은 것을 고르시오.

① 위로   ② 꾸중
③ 충고   ④ 축하

M Mom, I want to do better _____ _____ _____ .

W Good for you. _____ _____ _____ _____ going out with your friends so much.

M Yes, I know.

W Your friends, John and Paul, don't like to study _____ _____ .

M I agree with you. They just have fun all the time.

W So you _____ _____ _____ _____ with them.

15 대화를 듣고, 현재 시각으로 알맞은 것을 고르시오.

① 3:00
② 3:10
③ 3:20
④ 3:30

M Oh, I almost forgot. I have to go now. I'm going to meet Paul _____ _____ _____.

W What time will you meet him?

M I will meet him at 3:30.

W _____ _____ _____ _____ _____. Can you walk to the library in 20 minutes?

M Maybe, I can. But I think _____ _____ _____ _____ _____ right now and run.

W Take care. See you later.

---

16 대화를 듣고, 여자의 심경으로 가장 알맞은 것을 고르시오.

① angry
② sad
③ lonely
④ tired

M _____ _____ _____. What's wrong?

W I don't feel well. You know my dog, Sam? He is in the animal hospital.

M Oh, I'm sorry _____ _____ _____. Will he be OK?

W The doctor said _____ _____ _____ _____ because he is so old.

M That's too bad.

---

17 대화를 듣고, 여자의 언니에 대한 설명과 일치하지 않는 것을 고르시오.

① She got married.
② There are three people in her family.
③ Her daughter is one year old.
④ She has lived in Canada for five years.

M Oh, sorry. I'm a little late. Who were you talking to?

W My sister. She lives in Canada.

M _____ _____ _____ _____ to Canada?

W Five years ago. _____ _____ _____ _____ her husband and her daughter.

M How many children does she have?

W _____ _____.

18 다음을 듣고, 남부와 북부의 내일 날씨로 바르게 연결된 것을 고르시오.

① rainy – sunny
② sunny – rainy
③ rainy – rainy
④ sunny – sunny

M Good evening. This is the national weather report. The northern half of the country _____ _____ _____ than the southern part of the country. The south was rainy today. The north was sunny. But tomorrow _____ _____ _____ _____ _____ and the north will be rainy. So the people in the south will _____ _____ _____ .

19 대화를 듣고, 여자의 마지막 말에 이어질 남자의 응답으로 가장 적절한 것을 고르시오.

① That's too bad.
② You're welcome.
③ Don't worry about it.
④ That's a good idea.

M _____ _____ _____ .
W Me too. We got to the library at 1 o'clock. And now it's 5 o'clock.
M So we've been studying _____ _____ _____ _____ . We should take a break.
W OK. Let's go _____ _____ _____ .
M _____

20 대화를 듣고, 여자의 마지막 말에 이어질 남자의 응답으로 가장 적절한 것을 고르시오.

① I will congratulate him now.
② Thank you for helping me.
③ Your essay was really good.
④ I can't believe I won.

M Bob looks very happy. What happened?
W He _____ _____ _____ _____ . The teacher told our class this morning.
M Oh, that's good for him.
W Yes. He _____ _____ _____ _____ _____ writing his essay. He is happy he won.
M _____

1 다음을 듣고, 무엇에 관한 설명인지 고르시오.

①

②

③

④

2 대화를 듣고, 두 사람이 운동 삼아 하는 것에 속하지 <u>않는</u> 것을 고르시오.

① 수영　　　　　　② 야구
③ 산책　　　　　　④ 농구

3 대화를 듣고, 남자와 아들의 닮은 점이 <u>아닌</u> 것을 고르시오.

① 식성　　　　　　② 말투
③ 장래 희망　　　　④ 걸음걸이

4 다음을 듣고, 오늘 오후의 날씨로 예상되는 것을 고르시오.

①

②

③

④

5 대화를 듣고, 여자의 장래희망으로 알맞은 것을 고르시오.

① 과학자　　　　　② 생물학자
③ 의사　　　　　　④ 우주비행사

6 대화를 듣고, 여자가 마지막에 한 말의 의도를 고르시오.

① 동의　　　　　　② 염려
③ 제안　　　　　　④ 소망

7 대화를 듣고, 남자가 구입할 셔츠의 모양을 고르시오.

①

②

③

④

8 대화를 듣고, 남자가 패스트푸드점에서 하는 것이 <u>아닌</u> 것을 고르시오.

① 패스트푸드점에 가면 항상 햄버거를 먹는다.
② 일주일에 세 번 패스트푸드점에 간다.
③ 패스트푸드점에서 친구들과 이야기를 나눈다.
④ 감자튀김을 좋아하지 않는다.

9 대화를 듣고, 남자가 Kenny의 집에 가는 목적을 고르시오.

① 그의 책을 빌리러
② 같이 도서관에 가려고
③ 도서관에 반납할 책을 받으러
④ 도서관에서 빌린 책을 갖다 주러

10 대화를 듣고, 수리업자가 방문하기로 한 시각을 고르시오.

① 오늘 저녁 7시
② 내일 아침 10시
③ 내일 오후 2시
④ 내일 저녁 7시

11 다음을 듣고, 설문조사 결과의 내용과 일치하지 <u>않</u>는 것을 고르시오.

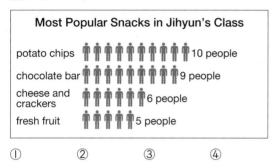

Most Popular Snacks in Jihyun's Class

potato chips 10 people
chocolate bar 9 people
cheese and crackers 6 people
fresh fruit 5 people

① ② ③ ④

12 다음을 듣고, 두 사람의 대화가 <u>어색한</u> 것을 고르시오.

① ② ③ ④

13 대화를 듣고, 남자가 지불해야 하는 금액을 고르시오.

① $2 ② $4 ③ $6 ④ $8

14 대화를 듣고, 대화가 이루어지는 장소를 고르시오.

① 호텔 ② 병원
③ 비행기 ④ 식당

15 대화를 듣고, 두 사람이 지금 할 일을 고르시오.

① 집에 가기
② 다른 영화관으로 가기
③ 영화표 예매하기
④ 상영관으로 들어가기

16 대화를 듣고, 남자가 좋아하는 색상이 <u>아닌</u> 것을 고르시오.

① 흰색 ② 파란색
③ 핑크색 ④ 검정색

17 다음 그림의 상황에 가장 알맞은 대화를 고르시오.

① ② ③ ④

18 대화를 듣고, 남자의 심경으로 가장 알맞은 것을 고르시오.

① worried
② satisfied
③ grateful
④ curious

[19-20] 대화를 듣고, 남자의 마지막 말에 이어질 여자의 응답으로 가장 적절한 것을 고르시오.

19
① Don't worry about it.
② Oh, I'm sorry to hear that.
③ Just a moment. I'll go and get him.
④ Please telephone him later.

20
① Come over here. Hurry up!
② What would you like to order?
③ Have a seat. The waiter will be here soon.
④ Come this way. I'll show you to your table.

1 다음을 듣고, 무엇에 관한 설명인지 고르시오.

① ② ③ ④

M People sleep on beds in this building. The people _____ _____ _____, though. They are sick. And _____ _____ _____ so that doctors and nurses can watch them carefully. When people become healthy, _____ _____ _____ _____ _____ this building.

2 대화를 듣고, 두 사람이 운동 삼아 하는 것에 속하지 <u>않는</u> 것을 고르시오.

① 수영
② 야구
③ 산책
④ 농구

M What do you do _____ _____?
W Not much. _____ _____ _____ _____ _____.
   What about you?
M I go swimming twice a week. And I play basketball every Saturday.
W Well, _____ _____ _____ _____ _____ four times a week.
M Is that all?
W Yes, I don't really like sports.

3 대화를 듣고, 남자와 아들의 닮은 점이 <u>아닌</u> 것을 고르시오.

① 식성
② 말투
③ 장래 희망
④ 걸음걸이

W Our son acts just like you.
M _____ _____ _____ _____?
W Yes. He walks and talks like you.
M Yes, I think so. And he said he wants to _____ _____ _____ _____, too.
W I know. Whenever I look at my son, I see you.
M He prefers meat, _____ _____ _____ vegetables.
W You're right. _____ _____ _____ _____ between you and him.

4 다음을 듣고, 오늘 오후의 날씨로 예상되는 것을 고르시오.

① ② ③ ④

M Good afternoon. This is Harry Hanson with the weather report. It is _____ _____ _____. Spring is here. It is _____ _____ _____. The windy weather will continue for the rest of the day. Tomorrow will be rainy. Your flowers _____ _____ _____ for the rain.

5 대화를 듣고, 여자의 장래희망으로 알맞은 것을 고르시오.
① 과학자
② 생물학자
③ 의사
④ 우주비행사

M Which science class are you going to take next year?
W _____. I will study about plants and animals.
M What kind of job do you want to have?
W I want to be a doctor. I hope I can _____ _____ _____ and go to medical school. How about you?
M I want to live _____ _____ _____ _____.
W Oh, an astronaut? That's cool.

6 대화를 듣고, 여자가 마지막에 한 말의 의도를 고르시오.
① 동의
② 염려
③ 제안
④ 소망

W Did you watch *the Laugh House Comedy Show* last night?
M _____ _____ _____ a TV in my house.
W Really? What do you do at night?
M People in my family usually read, talk and _____ _____ _____ a lot at night.
W I wish _____ _____ _____ _____ _____, too. I don't want to watch so much TV.

7 대화를 듣고, 남자가 구입할 셔츠의 모양을 고르시오.

① ② ③ ④

M I like _____ _____ _____.
W You like the white shirt with blue stripes?
M Yes, stripes are _____ _____ _____.
W But the shirt seems to be _____ _____ _____. I prefer the polka-dotted shirt. It's fashionable.
M No, thanks. I don't like polka dots. What about the black and white checked shirt?
W _____ _____ _____.
M OK. I'll get it.

8 대화를 듣고, 남자가 패스트푸드점에서 하는 것이 <u>아닌</u> 것을 고르시오.

① 패스트푸드점에 가면 항상 햄버거를 먹는다.
② 일주일에 세 번 패스트푸드점에 간다.
③ 패스트푸드점에서 친구들과 이야기를 나눈다.
④ 감자튀김을 좋아하지 않는다.

M I'm hungry. I want to eat a hamburger.
W You eat a lot of hamburgers.
M I don't think so. I go to fast food restaurants three times a week.
W Three times a week! _____ _____ _____. Fast food is not healthy.
M It's OK. I don't always eat hamburgers. I often _____ _____ _____ _____ and talk to my friends. _____ _____, I don't eat french fries.

9 대화를 듣고, 남자가 Kenny의 집에 가는 목적을 고르시오.

① 그의 책을 빌리러
② 같이 도서관에 가려고
③ 도서관에 반납할 책을 받으러
④ 도서관에서 빌린 책을 갖다 주러

M _____ _____ _____ now, Mom.
W Where are you going?
M I'm going to Kenny's house first.
W I thought you said you were going to the library.
M I will go to the library later. I am going to Kenny's house to _____ _____ _____ _____.
W Does he want you to _____ _____ _____ _____ to the library?
M Yes, he does. So I am going to his house to get the book.

10 대화를 듣고, 수리업자가 방문하기로 한 시각을 고르시오.

① 오늘 저녁 7시
② 내일 아침 10시
③ 내일 오후 2시
④ 내일 저녁 7시

W When _____ _____ _____ be here?
M Tomorrow afternoon. Around 2 o'clock.
W Can someone come in the morning?
M _____ _____ _____ in the morning.
W But I am busy tomorrow afternoon.
M OK. I'll send someone _____ _____ _____. Is 7 OK?
W Yes, 7 in the evening is fine.

11 다음을 듣고, 설문조사 결과의 내용과 일치하지 <u>않는</u> 것을 고르시오.

Most Popular Snacks in Jihyun's Class

potato chips ♟♟♟♟♟♟♟♟♟♟ 10 people
chocolate bar ♟♟♟♟♟♟♟♟ 8 people
cheese and crackers ♟♟♟♟♟♟ 6 people
fresh fruit ♟♟♟♟♟♟♟♟♟♟ 10 people

①   ②   ③   ④

M ① Potato chips are the most popular snack.
② Chocolate bars are _____ _____ _____ potato chips.
③ More students _____ _____ _____ than cheese and crackers.
④ _____ _____ like to have fresh fruit for a snack.

12 다음을 듣고, 두 사람의 대화가 <u>어색한</u> 것을 고르시오.

①　　　②　　　③　　　④

① **M** Did you finish your homework?

W I am doing it right now.

② **M** What kind of movies do you like?

W I go to the movies _____ _____ _____.

③ **M** The weather is _____ _____ _____ _____.

W Yes, it is. I hope we have a good time.

④ **M** _____ _____ _____ on my math test.

W _____ _____. You'll do better next time.

13 대화를 듣고, 남자가 지불해야 하는 금액을 고르시오.

① $2
② $4
③ $6
④ $8

M I'd like two hamburger meals, please.

W _____ _____ _____ _____. Would you like cola or something else?

M Cola, please.

W The meals are _____ _____.

M I have this coupon. If I buy one meal, I can _____ _____ _____ _____. Right?

W Yes, you can use it now.

14 대화를 듣고, 대화가 이루어지는 장소를 고르시오.

① 호텔
② 병원
③ 비행기
④ 식당

M We have a reservation.

W What is your name, sir?

M Matthew Sweet.

W Yes, here it is. Mr. Sweet. You _____ _____ _____ for six.

M Right, in the non-smoking section.

W Yes, it's in the non-smoking section. _____ _____ and I'll take you to your table. *[pause]* Here it is. _____ _____ _____.

15 대화를 듣고, 두 사람이 지금 할 일을 고르시오.

① 집에 가기
② 다른 영화관으로 가기
③ 영화표 예매하기
④ 상영관으로 들어가기

M The movie _____ _____ _____.

W Sold out?

M It's _____ _____ _____ tonight. We'll have to go home.

W Can we drive to another cinema?

M Good idea. The movie was showing at the Megabox 12, too. _____ _____ _____.

W Let's go there. I hope it's not too late.

16 대화를 듣고, 남자가 좋아하는 색상이 <u>아닌</u> 것을 고르시오.

① 흰색
② 파란색
③ 핑크색
④ 검정색

W You should wear the shirt _____ _____ _____.

M Hmm... I don't know about that.

W Why not?

M I rather want to wear something in blue or white.

W But you look really great _____ _____ _____ _____. Is that the color that bothers you?

M _____ _____ _____ with that color. I think black is okay, too.

W Black? You never wear black shirts, either.

M I do when I _____ _____ _____.

17 다음을 듣고, 그림의 상황에 가장 알맞은 대화를 고르시오.

①   ②   ③   ④

① **M** I have to remind you that _____ _____ _____ _____ next month.

   W Oh, yes. You told me last week.

② **M** Good afternoon, Sarah. Please come in. Thanks for coming.

   W Good afternoon, Mike. Thank you for _____ _____.

③ **M** Alice, have you planned anything for tomorrow?

   W Yes. I'm going to visit my aunt _____ _____.

④ **M** Excuse me, ma'am. _____ _____ _____ _____ the store.

   W Oh, I thought that you are open until 9:00 p.m.

18 대화를 듣고, 남자의 심경으로 가장 알맞은 것을 고르시오.

① worried
② satisfied
③ grateful
④ curious

W Your birthday is coming up. I have already _____ _____ _____.

M What is my birthday present, Mom?

W I can't tell you. I'll give it to you on that day.

M But I really want to know.

W Of course you really want to know. But I won't _____ _____ _____.

M Please. _____ _____ _____ _____ then. Is it a bike? A Nintendo game player?

19 대화를 듣고, 남자의 마지막 말에 이어질 여자의 응답으로 가장 적절한 것을 고르시오.

① Don't worry about it.
② Oh, I'm sorry to hear that.
③ Just a moment. I'll go and get him.
④ Please phone him later.

[Knock, Knock]

W _____ _____ _____?

M Hello, Mrs. Jones. Is Fred at home?

W Yes, he is. He is in his room.

M Can he come outside and play with me?

W If he wants. _____ _____ _____?

M Yes, _____ _____ _____ _____ the apartment. Could you ask him, please?

W _____

20 대화를 듣고, 남자의 마지막 말에 이어질 여자의 응답으로 가장 적절한 것을 고르시오.

① Come over here. Hurry up!
② What would you like to order?
③ Have a seat. The waiter will be here soon.
④ Come this way. I'll show you to your table.

W Good evening. How may I help you?

M We want a table for dinner.

W How many people are there _____ _____ _____?

M There are four people. _____ _____ and two children.

W OK. We have _____ _____ _____.

M That's good.

W _____

WORD AND EXPRESSION REVIEW • TEST 1-2

A Write down the definition of each word or phrase.

1	regular	11	community
2	annual	12	volunteer
3	musical instrument	13	prefer
4	borrow	14	grade
5	remind	15	astronaut
6	government	16	repairperson
7	overtake	17	include
8	environment	18	bother
9	pollution	19	comfortable
10	cough	20	available

B Match each word with the right definition.

1	judge	_____	a	~을 가득 채우다
2	release	_____	b	열다, 개최하다
3	degree	_____	c	연주, 연기, 상연
4	invite	_____	d	판사, 심판관, 심사원
5	get married	_____	e	개봉하다
6	reserve	_____	f	일행
7	fill up	_____	g	꺼리다, 싫어하다
8	hold	_____	h	결혼하다
9	mind	_____	i	그러나, 그렇지만
10	biology	_____	j	(온도 등의) ~도
11	performance	_____	k	생물학
12	though	_____	l	줄무늬, 줄, 줄무늬를 넣다
13	section	_____	m	예약을 하다, 지정하다
14	party	_____	n	구역, 지구
15	stripe	_____	o	~을 초대하다

C Choose the best answer for the blank.

1 Can you _____ me a ride?

    a. give   b. take   c. drive

2 They danced _____ the piano music.

    a. by   b. to   c. with

3 I _____ to read the newspaper, but I usually don't have time to read it.

    a. use to   b. used to   c. am used to

4 I am thankful to you _____ your help.

    a. to   b. with   c. for

5 He spent the weekend _____ TV.

    a. watch   b. watching   c. to watch

6 Excuse me, ma'am. We're about _____ the store.

    a. to close   b. closing   c. to closing

D Complete the short dialogues.

1 A: Excuse me, I _____ a reservation for tonight.

    B: Yes, may I have your name, please?

2 A: I like this shirt with black stripes.

    B: But it seems to be _____ _____ fashion.

3 A: I think we need to take a break. Why don't we take a walk?

    B: OK. Let's go _____ a walk.

4 A: I never wear skirts.

    B: I don't, _____.

5 A: How did you get to work today?

    B: Well, I got to work by subway, because there _____ too much snow.

1 다음을 듣고, 그림의 상황에 가장 알맞은 대화를 고르시오.

① ② ③ ④

2 다음을 듣고, 주로 무엇에 관한 내용인지 고르시오.
① skin cancer
② suntan lotion
③ outdoor activities
④ harmful sun exposure

3 대화를 듣고, 남자가 할 일을 고르시오.
① 참치 사오기
② 청소기 돌리기
③ 샌드위치 만들기
④ 거실에 장식하기

4 대화를 듣고, 내용과 일치하지 않는 것을 고르시오.
① 할머니는 팔을 다치셨다.
② 할머니는 건강이 좋아지고 있다.
③ 여자는 할머니에게 매일 찾아간다.
④ 여자는 할머니에게 빨리 나아지라고 계속 말하고 있다.

5 대화를 듣고, 여자가 점수가 잘 나오는 과목을 고르시오.
① history
② math
③ science
④ philosophy

6 대화를 듣고, 여자가 지불해야 할 금액을 고르시오.
① $3.00
② $3.50
③ $4.00
④ $4.50

7 다음을 듣고, 두 사람의 대화가 어색한 것을 고르시오.
① ② ③ ④

8 다음을 듣고, 내용에 가장 알맞은 안내문을 고르시오.
① DO NOT WASTE TIME
② LET'S PREVENT FIRE
③ LET'S SAVE MONEY
④ LET'S CONSERVE ENERGY

9 대화를 듣고, 남자의 현재 장래희망으로 알맞은 것을 고르시오.
① racing driver   ② mechanic
③ car designer   ④ car salesman

10 다음을 듣고, 내용과 일치하는 것을 고르시오.
① 준혁이는 캐나다로 여행을 갔다.
② 상현이는 준혁이에게 전화를 많이 했다.
③ 상현이는 준혁이에게 딱 한번 편지를 썼다.
④ 준혁이는 우정을 그다지 중요하게 생각하지 않았다.

11 대화를 듣고, 여자가 좋아하는 동물을 고르시오.

①   ②

③   ④

12 대화를 듣고, 남자가 여자에게 전화를 건 목적을 고르시오.

① 진료 예약을 하려고
② 진료 시간을 물어보려고
③ 지금 당장 가도 되는지 알아보려고
④ 사탕이 목에 걸려서, 응급처치를 받으려고

13 대화를 듣고, 여자와 남자가 말하고 있는 것을 고르시오.

① 만날 날짜 정하기
② 축구 시합일 정하기
③ 피아노 수업 날짜 정하기
④ 날씨가 화창한 날 알아보기

14 대화를 듣고, 남자가 하는 말의 의도로 알맞은 것을 고르시오.

① 충고
② 제안
③ 칭찬
④ 동의

15 대화를 듣고, 남자가 목적지에 도착하게 될 시각을 고르시오.

① 10시 30분
② 10시 45분
③ 11시 45분
④ 12시 30분

16 대화를 듣고, 남자의 심경으로 가장 알맞은 것을 고르시오.

① excited
② worried
③ upset
④ confident

17 대화를 듣고, 이어지는 질문에 답하시오.

① clothes
② science homework
③ science teacher
④ school festival

18 다음을 듣고, 오늘과 내일의 날씨로 바르게 연결된 것을 고르시오.

　　〈오늘〉　　〈내일〉
① 몹시 추움 － 눈이 내림
② 눈이 내림 － 몹시 추움
③ 영하 2도 － 영하 10도
④ 눈이 내림 － 조금 더 따뜻해짐

[19~20] 대화를 듣고, 남자의 마지막 말에 이어질 여자의 응답으로 가장 적절한 것을 고르시오.

19

① Two o'clock.
② On Saturday.
③ For two days.
④ For the second time.

20

① Vancouver is nice place to live.
② My vacation was wonderful.
③ Canada is very big.
④ I'm from Vancouver.

1 다음을 듣고, 그림의 상황에 가장 알맞은 대화를 고르시오.

① ② ③ ④

① **W** Do you have the time?

M _____ _____ _____ . We have to hurry and _____ _____ _____ .

② **W** Do you like the watch?

M Yes, how much is it?

③ **W** _____ _____ _____ . It's dangerous.

M Yes, I will be careful. _____ _____ is very heavy.

④ **W** Do you have the time?

M Sorry, I don't _____ _____ _____ .

---

2 다음을 듣고, 주로 무엇에 관한 내용인지 고르시오.

① skin cancer
② suntan lotion
③ outdoor activities
④ harmful sun exposure

M Everyone knows the sun causes _____ _____ . Before you go outside to play, you should put suntan lotion on your skin. And _____ _____ _____ in the sun too long. _____ _____ _____ is dangerous and you must be careful.

---

3 대화를 듣고, 남자가 할 일을 고르시오.

① 참치 사오기
② 청소기 돌리기
③ 샌드위치 만들기
④ 거실에 장식하기

W Now everything is almost ready.

M What else do _____ _____ _____ _____ before the party starts?

W We have to make some sandwiches.

M But I am _____ _____ _____ _____ .

W Then you can _____ _____ _____ . The living room must be clean.

M OK. I'll vacuum the floor in the living room.

W Thanks. Then I'll make some tuna sandwiches.

---

4 대화를 듣고, 내용과 일치하지 않는 것을 고르시오.

① 할머니는 팔을 다치셨다.
② 할머니는 건강이 좋아지고 있다.
③ 여자는 할머니에게 매일 찾아간다.
④ 여자는 할머니에게 빨리 나아지라고 계속 말하고 있다.

M How is your grandmother?

W She is fine. _____ _____ _____ _____ .

M You told me _____ _____ _____ _____ .

W Yes, she did. I call her every day. I keep telling her to get better soon. I will visit _____ _____ _____ _____ this weekend.

M Good for you.

5 대화를 듣고, 여자가 점수가 잘 나오는 과목을 고르시오.

① history
② math
③ science
④ philosophy

M What is your favorite subject?

W History. I like to learn about history. Aristotle once said that history tells us _____ _____ _____ _____ _____.

M So, do you get good grades in history?

W _____ _____. I get better grades in science.

M You just like history _____ _____ _____.

W That's right. How about you?

M My favorite subject is math, and I'm good at it.

6 대화를 듣고, 여자가 지불해야 할 금액을 고르시오.

① $3.00
② $3.50
③ $4.00
④ $4.50

M Do you want something to drink with that?

W Yes. I'll have a soda pop.

M What kind of soda pop? _____ _____ _____?

W Cola, please. Large.

M OK. That's a hamburger and french fries with a large cola.

W _____ _____.

M That'll be 4 dollars and 50 cents.

W Oh, I have _____ _____. Can I use it here?

M Sure. You will _____ _____ _____ and 50 cents.

7 다음을 듣고, 두 사람의 대화가 어색한 것을 고르시오.

①   ②   ③   ④

① **M** _____ _____ _____ do you want?

  W It's $3.

② **M** Do you like pizza?

  W Yes, I do. _____ _____ _____?

③ **M** Let's go to the beach.

  W That's a good idea. The weather is good today.

④ **M** Where is the bank?

  W _____ _____ _____ _____. Keep walking.

TEST

3

8 다음을 듣고, 내용에 가장 알맞은 안내문을 고르시오.

① DO NOT WASTE TIME
② LET'S PREVENT FIRE
③ LET'S SAVE MONEY
④ LET'S CONSERVE ENERGY

M When you leave a room, _____ _____ _____ _____.
And keep the heater in your house at 20 degrees. Doing these things will _____ _____. Electricity is very expensive these days. _____ _____ _____ _____. We must save it.

9 대화를 듣고, 남자의 현재 장래희망으로 알맞은 것을 고르시오.

① racing driver
② mechanic
③ car designer
④ car salesman

M I love cars. I want a job _____ _____ _____.
W Are you good at _____ _____ _____ engines?
M Yes, I am, but I don't want to _____ _____ _____.
W Then a _____ _____?
M No, I want to design the outside of the car. I like cool looking cars.

10 다음을 듣고, 내용과 일치하는 것을 고르시오.

① 준혁이는 캐나다로 여행을 갔다.
② 상현이는 준혁이에게 전화를 많이 했다.
③ 상현이는 준혁이에게 딱 한번 편지를 썼다.
④ 준혁이는 우정을 그다지 중요하게 생각하지 않았다.

M Sanghyun's friend, Junhyuk, moved to Canada. Before Junhyuk left Korea, Sanghyun told him that _____ _____ _____ to him a lot. But Sanghyun _____ _____ _____. When he didn't see his friend, he didn't think about him. _____ _____ _____ _____, Junhyuk doesn't think friends could be _____ _____ _____.

11 대화를 듣고, 여자가 좋아하는 동물을 고르시오.

①　　②　
③　　④　

M What is your favorite animal?
W Well, I like a tall animal with a really long neck.
M Oh, with a long nose?
W No, it has a really long neck and long legs. It eats the leaves _____ _____ _____ _____.
M Does it _____ _____ _____ on its body?
W That's right. What about you? What is your favorite animal?
M A lion: _____ _____ _____ _____. It is very strong and powerful.

12 대화를 듣고, 남자가 여자에게 전화를 건 목적을 고르시오.

① 진료 예약을 하려고
② 진료 시간을 물어보려고
③ 지금 당장 가도 되는지 알아보려고
④ 사탕이 목에 걸려서, 응급처치를 받으려고

[Telephone rings.]

W Hello. White Teeth Dental Office.

M This is Jimmy Jones. I _____ _____ _____.

W Oh, are you _____ _____?

M Yes, I _____ _____ _____. I was eating some hard candy. It really hurts. Can I come in right now?

W Of course, you can.

M Oh, thank you. See you soon.

13 대화를 듣고, 여자와 남자가 말하고 있는 것을 고르시오.

① 만날 날짜 정하기
② 축구 시합일 정하기
③ 피아노 수업 날짜 정하기
④ 날씨가 화창한 날 알아보기

M I'm busy on Thursday afternoon. I have soccer practice.

W But I have a piano lesson Wednesday afternoon.

M It's hard to _____ _____ _____ to meet.

W How about _____ _____?

M Yes, that is fine.

W Good. _____ _____ _____. I hope the weather will be fine and perhaps we could go on a picnic.

14 대화를 듣고, 남자가 하는 말의 의도로 알맞은 것을 고르시오.

① 충고
② 제안
③ 칭찬
④ 동의

M You are snowboarding very well.

W I think I look terrible. _____ _____ _____ _____ again.

M _____ _____ this is your first time snowboarding.

W Yes, it is.

M So you're doing OK. You cannot do it _____ _____ _____ _____.

W Thanks. I'm doing my best.

15 대화를 듣고, 남자가 목적지에 도착하게 될 시각을 고르시오.

① 10시 30분
② 10시 45분
③ 11시 45분
④ 12시 30분

W Good morning. How can I help you?

M How long does the bus take to Oakville?

W It takes two and a half hours.

M _____ _____ _____ _____. Is there an express bus, too? I want to get there quickly.

W Yes, and it only takes _____ _____ _____ _____. There is a bus that leaves at 10:00, is it OK?

M Yes, I'll _____ _____ _____ _____.

16 대화를 듣고, 남자의 심경으로 가장 알맞은 것을 고르시오.

① excited
② worried
③ upset
④ confident

W The weather forecast said that _____ _____ _____ _____ _____.

M Yes, one is. Maybe we should _____ _____.

W The reporter said the storm would not be bad.

M But it could be. The storm _____ _____ _____. The weather report is sometimes wrong.

W Don't worry. Let's drive to grandma's. It will be fine.

17 대화를 듣고, 이어지는 질문에 답하시오.

① clothes
② science homework
③ science teacher
④ school festival

M Who were you talking to for _____ _____ _____ _____ on the telephone?

W Cathy.

M Is she _____ _____?

W Yes, she is. I asked her about our science homework. Our science teacher gave us too much homework.

M Really? I think you were _____ _____ _____.

W _____ _____ _____. We were talking about the science homework.

Q What did the girl talk about on the telephone?

18 다음을 듣고, 오늘과 내일의 날씨로 바르게 연결된 것을 고르시오.

〈오늘〉	〈내일〉
① 몹시 추움	– 눈이 내림
② 눈이 내림	– 몹시 추움
③ 영하 2도	– 영하 10도
④ 눈이 내림	– 조금 더 따뜻해짐

W Good evening, MUM listeners. I'm Janet Smith. _____ _____ _____ _____ today. Temperatures were minus 10 degrees. But _____ _____ _____ _____. Temperatures will be minus 2 degrees. It will begin snowing in the afternoon. _____ _____ _____ for snowy weather.

19 대화를 듣고, 남자의 마지막 말에 이어질 여자의 응답으로 가장 적절한 것을 고르시오.

① Two o'clock.
② On Saturday.
③ For two days.
④ For the second time.

M Do you _____ _____ _____ for this weekend?
W Yes, I do.
M Are you going somewhere?
W Yes, I'm going to visit my grandmother _____ _____ _____.
M _____ _____ _____ to see you.
W Yes, I think so. And I'll be happy to see her.
M How long will you stay with her?
W _____

20 대화를 듣고, 남자의 마지막 말에 이어질 여자의 응답으로 가장 적절한 것을 고르시오.

① Vancouver is nice place to live.
② My vacation was wonderful.
③ Canada is very big.
④ I'm from Vancouver.

M Hello. Nice to meet you.
W Hello. Glad to meet you, too.
M _____ _____ _____ _____?
W Canada.
M Oh, that's nice. Canada is very beautiful. I went to Toronto _____ _____ _____ _____ for a vacation. _____ _____ _____ Canada are you from?
W _____

1 다음을 듣고, 그림을 가장 적절하게 묘사한 것을 고르시오.

①   ②   ③   ④

2 다음을 듣고, 어제와 오늘의 날씨로 바르게 짝지어진 것을 고르시오.

3 대화를 듣고, 대화가 이루어지는 장소로 알맞은 것을 고르시오.
① 주차장
② 세차장
③ 톨게이트
④ 자동차 정비소

4 대화를 듣고, 여자가 공원에서 한 일을 고르시오.
① riding a bike
② doing in-line skating
③ taking a walk
④ having a lunch box

5 다음을 듣고, 무엇에 관한 안내인지 고르시오.
① 특별 세일 안내
② 1층 매장 안내
③ 선글라스 경품 행사 안내
④ 명품 선글라스 광고

6 다음을 듣고, 남자의 장래희망으로 알맞은 것을 고르시오.
① athlete
② farmer
③ salesperson
④ businessman

7 다음을 듣고, 두 사람의 대화가 어색한 것을 고르시오.
①   ②   ③   ④

8 대화를 듣고, 여자가 남자에게 전화를 건 목적을 고르시오.
① 몸은 좀 좋아졌는지 알아보려고
② 3일간 학교에 결석한다고 말하려고
③ 내일 어디서 만날 것인지 물어보려고
④ 내일은 학교에 간다고 말하려고

9 다음을 듣고, 상황에 어울리는 속담으로 알맞은 것을 고르시오.
① Easy come, easy go.
② Every dog has his day.
③ Make hay while the sun shines.
④ Don't count your chickens before they hatch.

10 다음을 듣고, 지금 무대에 펼쳐질 공연으로 알맞은 것을 고르시오.
① 춤   ② 노래
③ 연극   ④ 기타 연주

11 대화를 듣고, 남자가 가장 좋아하는 음식을 고르시오.

①
②
③
④

12 다음을 듣고, 시험지를 제출한 사람이 해야 할 일을 고르시오.

① 퇴실한다.
② 엎드려 있다.
③ 자리에 앉아 있다.
④ 시험지를 반으로 접어놓는다.

13 다음을 듣고, 마지막 질문에 가장 알맞은 답을 고르시오.

① I'll talk to you later.
② Can you hold on a second?
③ She is waiting for you in her room.
④ Just a moment... I'm afraid we're fully booked.

14 다음을 듣고, 표의 내용과 일치하지 <u>않는</u> 것을 고르시오.

	Sumin	Dabin	Junghyun
Age	13	12	14
Weight	40kg	52kg	44kg
Height	166cm	170cm	168cm

①　　　　②　　　　③　　　　④

15 대화를 듣고, 약속시간에 맞추기 위해 출발해야 할 시각을 고르시오.

① 6:30　　　　② 7:00
③ 7:30　　　　④ 8:00

16 대화를 듣고, 남자가 하는 말의 의도로 알맞은 것을 고르시오.

① 위로　　② 홍보　　③ 핀잔　　④ 조언

17 다음을 듣고, 도표의 내용과 일치하지 <u>않는</u> 것을 고르시오.

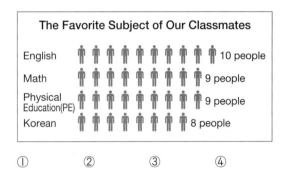

①　　　　②　　　　③　　　　④

18 대화를 듣고, 남자의 기분으로 알맞은 것을 고르시오.

① bored
② relaxed
③ nervous
④ exhausted

[19-20] 대화를 듣고, 남자의 마지막 말에 이어질 여자의 응답으로 가장 적절한 것을 고르시오.

19

① OK. I'll have it.
② Can I have dessert, please?
③ I'll have it well-done.
④ I'll have coffee now.

20

① Please be careful, then.
② Sit down and eat some corn.
③ You don't have to stand up.
④ Dinner will be a minute.

DICTATION • TEST 4

1 다음을 듣고, 그림을 가장 적절하게 묘사한 것을 고르시오.

① ② ③ ④

M ① A boy is _____ _____ _____.

② A father and his son are playing soccer.

③ A father and his son are _____ _____ _____ _____.

④ A father and his son are _____ _____ a beach.

2 다음을 듣고, 어제와 오늘의 날씨로 바르게 짝지어진 것을 고르시오.

〈어제〉–〈오늘〉　　〈어제〉–〈오늘〉
① ②
③ ④

W Good morning. This is the WWRK weather report. _____ _____. It's snowing. _____ _____ _____ at 2 a.m. and it's still snowing. Many schools will be closed. _____ _____ _____ _____. Yesterday the weather was rainy, so all this snow is a big change. Be careful if you drive today.

3 대화를 듣고, 대화가 이루어지는 장소로 알맞은 것을 고르시오.

① 주차장
② 세차장
③ 톨게이트
④ 자동차 정비소

M How much does it _____ _____ _____?

W It is $3 an hour. How many hours do you want to _____ _____ _____ _____?

M About 3 hours.

W OK. Park your car over there. _____ _____ _____ _____. Keep it in your car, please.

M OK. Thank you.

W And please remember to _____ _____ _____.

4 대화를 듣고, 여자가 공원에서 한 일을 고르시오.

① riding a bike
② doing in-line skating
③ taking a walk
④ having a lunch box

M What did you do at the park after lunch?

W We wanted to ride bikes, but we _____ _____ _____.

M Oh, that's too bad. Did you just _____ _____ _____, then?

W No, we could rent in-line skates. So we rented them and _____ _____ _____.

M Sounds like fun.

W It was. But I fell down a lot.

36 ● 위아 중학듣기 모의고사

5 다음을 듣고, 무엇에 관한 안내인지 고르시오.

① 특별 세일 안내
② 1층 매장 안내
③ 선글라스 경품 행사 안내
④ 명품 선글라스 광고

W Hello, shoppers. Sunglasses are now on sale. _____ _____ _____, sunglasses will be 40% off. It's a special sale only for one hour. _____ _____ _____ _____ will be on sale. Hurry to _____ _____ _____ before they are sold out.

6 다음을 듣고, 남자의 장래희망으로 알맞은 것을 고르시오.

① athlete
② farmer
③ salesperson
④ businessman

M I love working outside. I don't think I could _____ _____ _____ at a desk all day. So I want to _____ _____ and raise animals. I am trying to think of a good plant or crop to grow. I want to _____ _____ _____ that I can sell outside my country.

7 다음을 듣고, 두 사람의 대화가 어색한 것을 고르시오.

①   ②   ③   ④

① **M** Can you help me?
  W I'm afraid I can't. I'm very busy now.
② **M** Are you interested in movies?
  W Yes. _____ _____ _____.
③ **M** What a nice picture! _____ _____ _____.
  W I'm glad you like it.
④ **M** _____ _____ _____. What's the matter?
  W I got a good grade on the exam.

8 대화를 듣고, 여자가 남자에게 전화를 건 목적을 고르시오.

① 몸은 좀 좋아졌는지 알아보려고
② 3일간 학교에 결석한다고 말하려고
③ 내일 어디서 만날 것인지 물어보려고
④ 내일은 학교에 간다고 말하려고

[Telephone rings.]
M Hello.
W Hello. Hi, Jason, it's Lisa. Are you feeling better?
M Yes. _____ _____ _____. I will be at school tomorrow.
W That's good. We were getting worried about you. _____ _____ _____ _____ of school due to a bad cold.
M Well, _____ _____ _____ _____ tomorrow. Thank you.
W Good. See you tomorrow.

9 다음을 듣고, 상황에 어울리는 속담으로 알맞은 것을 고르시오.

① Easy come, easy go.
② Every dog has his day.
③ Make hay while the sun shines.
④ Don't count your chickens before they hatch.

M Jaewon knew exams were not close. Exams were three weeks away. But he _____ _____ anyway. He read his notes. _____ _____ _____ _____. The next week he got very sick. It took him a long time to get better. When he was better, he was happy _____ _____ _____ before he got sick.

10 다음을 듣고, 지금 무대에 펼쳐질 공연으로 알맞은 것을 고르시오.

① 춤
② 노래
③ 연극
④ 기타 연주

W Good evening, everyone. _____ _____ _____, the Flying Guitars, is getting ready. Before the Flying Guitars come out, a new singer will _____ _____ _____ _____. Her name is Gail Jones. She is a big star in Europe, but she _____ _____ _____ _____ in America. We hope you enjoy her beautiful voice.

11 대화를 듣고, 남자가 가장 좋아하는 음식을 고르시오.

①   ②

③   ④

M What type of fast food _____ _____ _____? Western food or Korean food?
W It doesn't matter.
M Well, my favorite fast food is a Korean dish. _____ _____ _____ what it is. It's long and round.
W _____ _____, right?
M No, it's dark green on the outside. Then _____ _____ _____ is white.
W Oh, I know what it is. It has meat and vegetables in the middle.
M Yes, it does.

T E S T

4

12 다음을 듣고, 시험지를 제출한 사람이 해야 할 일을 고르시오.

① 퇴실한다.
② 엎드려 있는다.
③ 자리에 앉아 있는다.
④ 시험지를 반으로 접어놓는다.

M Now, it's time to test you _____ _____ _____. When you finish your test, _____ _____ _____ _____. Then go back and sit down. You cannot leave the room. You must stay at your desk. When _____ _____ _____, you can leave the room. Thank you. _____ _____, please!

13 다음을 듣고, 마지막 질문에 가장 알맞은 답을 고르시오.

① I'll talk to you later.
② Can you hold on a second?
③ She is waiting for you in her room.
④ Just a moment... I'm afraid we're fully booked.

W The phone rings. It is someone who wants to talk to your sister. Your sister is _____ _____ _____. You tell the person on the phone that you will _____ _____ _____ _____. You want to tell _____ _____ _____ _____. What would you say in this situation?

14 다음을 듣고, 표의 내용과 일치하지 않는 것을 고르시오.

	Sumin	Dabin	Junghyun
Age	13	12	14
Weight	40kg	52kg	44kg
Height	166cm	170cm	168cm

① ② ③ ④

M ① Jeonghyun is older than Sumin _____ _____ _____.
② Sumin is the youngest, _____, _____ _____.
③ Dabin is the heaviest _____ _____ _____.
④ Jeonghyun is shorter than Dabin by 2cm.

15 대화를 듣고, 약속시간에 맞추기 위해 출발해야 할 시각을 고르시오.

① 6:30
② 7:00
③ 7:30
④ 8:00

M When do _____ _____ _____ _____ at Jane's house?

W 7:30. Aren't you hungry? Maybe we will _____ _____ _____ _____.

M It's 6:30 now. Do we have to _____ _____ _____?

W No, we don't have to hurry.

M How long does it take to go to Jane's house?

W _____ _____.

16 대화를 듣고, 남자가 하는 말의 의도로 알맞은 것을 고르시오.

① 위로
② 홍보
③ 핀잔
④ 조언

M Do you _____ _____ _____ _____?

W Yes, I do. I have had a cold for five days.

M I think you should take some rest. Oh, why don't you _____ _____ _____?

W Vitamins? Are vitamins good for our health?

M Yes, they keep you strong and healthy. You can buy some _____ _____ _____.

17 다음을 듣고, 도표의 내용과 일치하지 <u>않는</u> 것을 고르시오.

The Favorite Subject of Our Classmates	
English	♦♦♦♦♦♦♦♦♦♦ 10 people
Math	♦♦♦♦♦♦♦♦♦ 9 people
Physical Education(PE)	♦♦♦♦♦♦♦♦♦ 9 people
Korean	♦♦♦♦♦♦♦♦ 8 people

①　　②　　③　　④

W ① The subject _____ _____ _____ is English.

② PE is the favorite subject among the students.

③ Korean is _____ _____ _____ _____ among the students.

④ _____ _____ _____ _____ _____ PE.

18 대화를 듣고, 남자의 기분으로 알맞은 것을 고르시오.

① bored
② relaxed
③ nervous
④ exhausted

W Did you _____ _____ _____ _____ all day?

M _____ _____. I watched TV and played computer games.

W It's OK to relax today.

M Thanks. My exams ended yesterday and _____ _____ _____ _____.

W Well, tomorrow you have to start studying again.

M Mom! Don't make my good feeling _____ _____.

19 대화를 듣고, 남자의 마지막 말에 이어질 여자의 응답으로 가장 적절한 것을 고르시오.

① OK. I'll have it.
② Can I have dessert, please?
③ I'll have it well-done.
④ I'll have coffee now.

M May I take your order?

W Yes. What is today's special?

M _____ _____ _____ _____. Salmon with potatoes and vegetables.

W Umm... Is it delicious?

M It is. It's a _____ _____ _____ at this restaurant.

W _____

20 대화를 듣고, 남자의 마지막 말에 이어질 여자의 응답으로 가장 적절한 것을 고르시오.

① Please be careful, then.
② Sit down and eat some corn.
③ You don't have to stand up.
④ Dinner will be a minute.

W Tony, please come here.

M Yes, Mom. What do you want?

W I want the can of corn on the top shelf of _____ _____ _____.

M The can of corn _____ _____ _____ _____?

W Yes, I can't reach it.

M Oh, it's too high for me, too. I'll have to _____ _____ _____ _____.

W _____

WORD AND EXPRESSION REVIEW • TEST 3-4

A Write down the definition of each word or phrase.

1	watch out	11	temperature
2	luggage	12	chase
3	cause	13	fall down
4	activity	14	crop
5	harmful	15	grateful
6	console	16	vegetable
7	electricity	17	height
8	waste	18	healthy
9	involve	19	pharmacy
10	emergency	20	salmon

B Match each word with the right definition.

1	assume	a	타다, 탑승하다, 승차하다
2	discard	b	노출, 드러냄
3	fix	c	(신체를) 다치게 하다, 아픔을 주다
4	lie	d	아주 좋아하는
5	conserve	e	막다, 예방하다
6	raise	f	보호하다, 절약하다
7	exposure	g	고치다, 수리하다
8	board	h	수리공, 정비사, 기계공
9	hurt	i	버리다, 폐기하다
10	prevent	j	추측하다
11	kind of	k	(비용, 대가가 얼마) 들다
12	mechanic	l	기르다, 재배하다, 사육하다
13	cost	m	빠뜨리다, (수업에) 결석하다
14	favorite	n	눕다
15	miss	o	어느 정도, 약간, 얼마간

C Choose the best answer for the blank.

1 I keep _____ her to get better soon.

   a. tell   b. to tell   c. telling

2 Who is the tallest _____ you three?

   a. between   b. among   c. during

3 I was absent from school _____ to a bad cold.

   a. due   b. because   c. reason

4 My favorite subject is English, and I'm good _____ it.

   a. at   b. in   c. of

5 It _____ fun.

   a. sounds   b. sounds like   c. sounds to

6 Many people say coffee is bad for health. But on _____ it's good for relieving stress.

   a. other hands   b. the other hand   c. another hand

D Complete the short dialogues.

1 A: Mom, my hands are dry.

   B: _____ some lotion on your hands.

2 A: May I speak to Mary, please?

   B: _____ on a second.

3 A: Is this ring now on sale?

   B: Yes, it is 40% _____ now.

4 A: What is your favorite subject in your school?

   B: I like math the _____.

5 A: How much does it _____ per hour?

   B: It is $3 an hour.

1 다음을 듣고, 스승의 날에 재미있었던 일로 알맞은 것을 고르시오.

① 초코파이를 쌓다가 와르르 무너졌다.
② 선생님이 케이크를 한 번에 다 먹었다.
③ 선생님께 드린 파이를 학생들이 다 먹었다.
④ 선생님 얼굴에 케이크를 묻혔다.

2 대화를 듣고, 여자의 직업으로 알맞은 것을 고르시오.

① singer
② actress
③ director
④ show hostess

3 다음을 듣고, 남자가 설명하는 나라를 고르시오.

① Austria
② New Zealand
③ England
④ Australia

4 대화를 듣고, 여자의 마지막 말의 의도를 고르시오.

① 칭찬
② 소망
③ 위로
④ 제안

5 대화를 듣고, 남자가 찾는 곳을 고르시오.

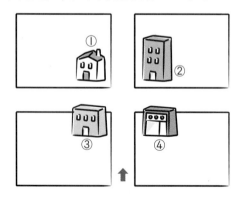

6 대화를 듣고, 여자가 마시지 <u>않는</u> 것을 고르시오.

① 콜라
② 차
③ 우유
④ 오렌지 주스

7 대화를 듣고, 남자가 전화를 한 목적을 고르시오.

① 이제 집에 간다고 말하려고
② 좀더 놀아도 되는지 물어보려고
③ 피아노 레슨 시간을 물어보려고
④ 축구시합 때문에 피아노 레슨을 미루어야 한다고

8 대화를 듣고, 여자가 남자보다 먼저 태어난 개월 수를 고르시오.

① 3 months
② 9 months
③ 12 months
④ 15 months

9 대화를 듣고, 남자가 대화 후 바로 하게 될 일을 고르시오.

① 짐 싸기
② 환전하기
③ 비행기 탑승수속
④ 호텔 입실 절차

10 다음을 듣고, 두 사람의 대화가 <u>어색한</u> 것을 고르시오.

①   ②   ③   ④

11 대화를 듣고, 두 사람이 만날 날로 알맞은 것을 고르시오.

DECEMBER						
SUN	MON	TUE	WED	THU	FRI	SAT
		1	2	3	4	5
6	7	8	9	10	11	12
13	14	15	16	17	18	19
20	21	22	23	24	25	26
27	28	29	30			

① 15일　　② 20일　　③ 22일　　④ 25일

12 대화를 듣고, 여자가 지불하게 될 금액을 고르시오.
① $25　　② $35　　③ $40　　④ $45

13 대화를 듣고, 여자의 심정으로 알맞은 것을 고르시오.
① scared　　　　② angry
③ excited　　　　④ surprised

14 대화를 듣고, 대화가 이루어지는 장소를 고르시오.
① bank　　　　② hotel
③ post office　　④ subway station

15 대화를 듣고, 남자가 해야 할 일을 고르시오.
① 우산을 산다.　　② 지하철을 탄다.
③ 택시를 기다린다.　④ 여자를 데리러 간다.

16 다음을 듣고, 그림의 상황에 가장 알맞은 대화를 고르시오.

①　　　②　　　③　　　④

17 대화를 듣고, 두 사람의 관계로 알맞은 것을 고르시오.
① 리포터 – 선수
② 취재 기자 – 영화 배우
③ 심판 – 축구 감독
④ 영화 감독 – 기자

18 대화를 듣고, 대화의 내용과 일치하지 <u>않는</u> 것을 고르시오.
① 여자는 3번 문제를 못 푼다.
② 여자는 1번과 2번 문제를 풀었다.
③ 남자는 여자에게 3번 문제를 가르쳐준다.
④ 여자는 남자에게 1번과 2번 문제를 가르쳐준다.

[19-20] 대화를 듣고, 여자의 마지막 말에 이어질 남자의 응답으로 가장 적절한 것을 고르시오.

19
① I hope I can go with him.
② The tickets are expensive.
③ We will have fun together.
④ Thank you for inviting me.

20
① Good night. See you in the morning.
② The doctor will see you now.
③ I hope you get better soon.
④ You should take some medicine.

1 다음을 듣고, 스승의 날에 재미있었던 일로 알맞은 것을 고르시오.

① 초코파이를 쌓다가 와르르 무너졌다.
② 선생님이 케이크를 한번에 다 먹었다.
③ 선생님께 드린 파이를 학생들이 다 먹었다.
④ 선생님 얼굴에 케이크를 묻혔다.

M Today was Teacher's Day. We made a chocolate pie cake for our teacher. _____ _____ _____ one chocolate pie. We _____ _____ _____ out of 36 small chocolate pies. Then we sang a song and gave the cake to the teacher. _____ _____ _____ was that the students ate the chocolate pies. The teacher _____ _____ _____.

2 대화를 듣고, 여자의 직업으로 알맞은 것을 고르시오.

① singer
② actress
③ director
④ show hostess

M Is this your first movie?

W No, it's _____ _____ _____.

M Oh, what was the name of your first movie?

W *Summer Romance*. My character was a friend of _____ _____ _____. I was a singer in the movie. It was a small part. But I learned a lot _____ _____ _____ of the movie.

M Your performance _____ _____ _____ _____. A lot of people thought you are a great singer.

W Nice to hear that.

3 다음을 듣고, 남자가 설명하는 나라를 고르시오.

① Austria
② New Zealand
③ England
④ Australia

M This country is _____ _____ _____ country in the world. The country _____ _____ _____ _____, but it is not considered an island. _____ _____ _____ _____. The central part of the country is called the Outback. And it is _____ _____. The people who live in this country speak English. Also, there is a world-famous Opera House.

4 대화를 듣고, 여자의 마지막 말의 의도를 고르시오.

① 칭찬
② 소망
③ 위로
④ 제안

W Look! That's that actress from the movie *Big Killer*.

M Yes, Alicia Stone. Do you want to go and meet her?

W No, _____ _____ _____ _____ . I am sure she needs her privacy. But she is _____ _____ _____ I thought.

M Don't worry you're tall, too.

W But I want to be even taller. Then I _____ _____ _____ _____ myself.

5 대화를 듣고, 남자가 찾는 곳을 고르시오.

① ② ③ ④

M Excuse me. Where is the Majestic Theater?

W Oh, you're very close to it.

M Oh, really? _____ _____ _____ _____ _____ . Can you tell me how to get there?

W Walk for one block and _____ _____ _____ _____ . It's on the left side.

M Walk for one block. Go across the street. _____ _____ _____ _____ _____ .

W That's right. You can't miss it.

6 대화를 듣고, 여자가 마시지 <u>않는</u> 것을 고르시오.

① 콜라
② 차
③ 우유
④ 오렌지 주스

M Do you want some coke?

W Make it diet coke. I'm _____ _____ _____ _____ .

M Well, I don't have _____ _____ _____ . How about some milk?

W That is one thing I really _____ _____ _____ .

M You're so strange. Have some juice then. I have tomato juice.

W Tomato? Oh, no. Do you have some orange juice?

M I do. Well, I will _____ _____ _____ for myself.

7 대화를 듣고, 남자가 전화를 한 목적을 고르시오.

① 이제 집에 간다고 말하려고
② 좀더 놀아도 되는지 물어보려고
③ 피아노 레슨 시간을 물어보려고
④ 축구시합 때문에 피아노 레슨을 미루어야 한다고

[Telephone rings.]

W Hello.

M Hello, Mom. It's me. I'm at school.

W _____ _____ _____ _____ home? I'm waiting for you.

M I am playing soccer with my friends. Can I play _____ _____ _____ _____ ?

W OK. _____ _____ _____ . You have piano lessons later this afternoon.

M Thanks, Mom. I'll play for 30 minutes more and then come home.

W Good. See you then.

8 대화를 듣고, 여자가 남자보다 먼저 태어난 개월 수를 고르시오.

① 3 months
② 9 months
③ 12 months
④ 15 months

M I was _____ _____ _____ and you were born in September.

W So I am _____ _____ _____ than you are.

M Let's see... I was born on the 5th of December 1994.

W 1994? I was born _____ _____ _____ _____ _____ 1993.

M 1993! You're one year and 3 months older than me.

9 대화를 듣고, 남자가 대화 후 바로 하게 될 일을 고르시오.

① 짐 싸기
② 환전하기
③ 비행기 탑승수속
④ 호텔 입실 절차

W Did you _____ _____ _____ ?

M Yes, I did.

W Good. You'll be ready when you get there. Are you hungry?

M Not at all. _____ _____ _____ _____ , Mom. I have to go now.

W OK. _____ _____ _____ up to the counter. [pause] I'm sure going to miss you.

M I'll miss you, too, Mom. I'll call you when I get there.

10 다음을 듣고, 두 사람의 대화가 <u>어색한</u> 것을 고르시오.

① ② ③ ④

① **W** What's wrong? You look so sad.

M _____ _____ _____ this morning.

② **W** Can you come over to my place?

M What time do you want _____ _____ _____ _____ ?

③ **W** Traffic is slow. Was there an accident?

M No, ma'am. It's just _____ _____ _____ .

④ **W** What are you doing now?

M I played soccer after school.

11 대화를 듣고, 두 사람이 만날 날로 알맞은 것을 고르시오.

DECEMBER						
SUN	MON	TUE	WED	THU	FRI	SAT
		1	2	3	4	5
6	7	8	9	10	11	12
13	14	15	16	17	18	19
20	21	22	23	24	25	26
27	28	29	30			

① 15일 ② 20일
③ 22일 ④ 25일

M Monday and Tuesday are good nights for me to _____ _____ _____.

W Are you busy on the weekends?

M Yes, I work in a restaurant on weekends.

W What about _____ _____ _____ in December?

M One week later is better for me. I _____ _____ _____ _____ _____ and I want to treat you.

W OK. That will be a nice _____ _____ _____.

12 대화를 듣고, 여자가 지불하게 될 금액을 고르시오.

① $25
② $35
③ $40
④ $45

M Let's see. Your haircut was $25. And your son's hair cut was $15.

W Oh, wait a second. I think I have a coupon _____ _____.

M OK. [pause]

W Yes, here it is. It's a coupon for $10 off.

M Can I see it, please? I'm sorry, ma'am. _____ _____ _____. It was good until last month. You can't use it.

W Oh, I didn't know that the coupon had _____ _____ _____ _____.

13 대화를 듣고, 여자의 심정으로 알맞은 것을 고르시오.

① scared
② angry
③ excited
④ surprised

W Turn it off! I think I told you 20 minutes ago.

M Just a minute, Mom. _____ _____ _____.

W _____ _____ _____ if you're finished or not. Turn it off right now!

M Hold on. I will. I know I have to go to swimming lessons.

W Ted, if you do not _____ _____ _____ _____ _____, I will come in there and turn it off myself!

14 대화를 듣고, 대화가 이루어지는 장소를 고르시오.

① bank
② hotel
③ post office
④ subway station

W Good morning, sir. How may I help you?

M I'd like to _____ _____ _____.

W Did you _____ _____ _____ _____?

M Yes, I did while waiting for my turn.

W Can I have your _____ _____?

M Here it is.

W Thank you. [pause] Here you go, sir.

M Thank you. Well, could you tell me where the post office is?

15 대화를 듣고, 남자가 해야 할 일을 고르시오.

① 우산을 산다.
② 지하철을 탄다.
③ 택시를 기다린다.
④ 여자를 데리러 간다.

[Telephone rings.]

M Hello.

W Hello, Paul. This is Ally. Are you busy?

M No, not really. I'm just watching TV.

W _____ _____ _____ _____ the subway station and pick me up? I have _____ _____ _____ _____ _____.

M Sure. Do you have an umbrella?

W No, I don't.

M _____ _____ _____ in a few minutes.

16 다음을 듣고, 그림의 상황에 가장 알맞은 대화를 고르시오.

①   ②   ③   ④

① **W** _____ _____ _____ _____ _____. Let's go for a walk.

   M Okay, _____ _____ _____ _____ my brown jacket.

② **W** Sharon told me that _____ _____ _____. Is that right?

   M Yeah, I've loved biking since I was a child.

③ **W** How would you like _____ _____ _____? Medium or well-done?

   M Well-done, please.

④ **W** Here we go! What should we buy _____ _____ _____?

   M How about getting some snacks or fruit?

17 대화를 듣고, 두 사람의 관계로 알맞은 것을 고르시오.

① 리포터 – 선수
② 취재 기자 – 영화 배우
③ 심판 – 축구 감독
④ 영화 감독 – 기자

W Congratulations! You were voted _____ _____ _____ _____ of the game.

M Thank you. _____ _____ _____.

W Can you _____ _____ _____ about your goal?

M My goal... Bobby Fisher, our mid-fielder made a great pass. _____ _____ _____ _____ _____.

W It was a great goal, wasn't it?

M Thanks.

18 대화를 듣고, 대화의 내용과 일치하지 <u>않는</u> 것을 고르시오.

① 여자는 3번 문제를 못 푼다.
② 여자는 1번과 2번 문제를 풀었다.
③ 남자는 여자에게 3번 문제를 가르쳐준다.
④ 여자는 남자에게 1번과 2번 문제를 가르쳐준다.

W Did you _____ _____ number 3?
M Yes, I did. I've finished all my homework.
W Oh, good. Can you show me _____ _____ _____ _____?
M _____ _____ _____ _____ with questions 1 and 2?
W No, they were easy for me.
M OK. I will show you how to solve it.

19 대화를 듣고, 여자의 마지막 말에 이어질 남자의 응답으로 가장 적절한 것을 고르시오.

① I hope I can go with him.
② The tickets are expensive.
③ We will have fun together.
④ Thank you for inviting me.

M I wanted to _____ _____ _____ _____ this weekend.
W And is there a problem?
M Yes, the tickets are _____ _____ _____.
W Sold out? You mean the Mariah Carey concert?
M Yes, I love her. I really want to go to the concert.
W Well, I heard that Phillip has _____ _____ _____.
M _____

20 대화를 듣고, 여자의 마지막 말에 이어질 남자의 응답으로 가장 적절한 것을 고르시오.

① Good night. See you in the morning.
② The doctor will see you now.
③ I hope you get better soon.
④ You should take some medicine.

W [Coughing, Coughing] Oh, I don't feel well.
M _____ _____ _____ you have a cold.
W I do. _____ _____ _____ _____.
M Did you take some medicine?
W Yes, I did. But it doesn't work. I'm going home now _____ _____ _____ _____.
M _____

1 다음을 듣고, 그림의 상황에 가장 알맞은 대화를 고르시오.

①   ②   ③   ④

2 다음을 듣고, 무엇에 관한 내용인지 고르시오.
① takeoff
② landing
③ boarding
④ seat belt

3 대화를 듣고, 대화 직후 여자가 할 일을 고르시오.
① 쇼핑하기
② 집으로 가기
③ 사진관에서 기다리기
④ 커피숍에서 기다리기

4 대화를 듣고, 내용과 일치하지 않는 것을 고르시오.
① 할아버지 댁은 여자네 집에서 가깝다.
② 할머니는 음식을 여자에게 갖다 주신다.
③ 할머니는 음식을 많이 만드신다.
④ 여자는 할아버지와 할머니를 한 달에 서너 번 만난다.

5 대화를 듣고, 여자가 남자에게 읽기를 바라는 뉴스를 고르시오.
① 국내면
② 정치면
③ 국제면
④ 스포츠면

6 대화를 듣고, 두 사람이 현재 있는 장소를 고르시오.
① art museum
② concert hall
③ library
④ photograph shop

7 다음을 듣고, 두 사람의 대화가 어색한 것을 고르시오.
①   ②   ③   ④

8 다음을 듣고, 내용에 가장 알맞은 안내문을 고르시오.
① DON'T TOUCH THE ANIMALS
② BE CAREFUL OF WILD ANIMALS
③ FASTEN YOUR SEAT BELT
④ DON'T GIVE FOOD TO THE ANIMALS

9 대화를 듣고, 여자의 직업으로 알맞은 것을 고르시오.
① cook
② cashier
③ waitress
④ housewife

10 대화를 듣고, 두 사람이 쇼핑하러 가는 이유를 고르시오.
① 엄마의 생신 선물을 교환하러
② 각자 엄마의 생신 선물을 사기 위해서
③ 엄마에게 받은 책 생일 선물을 교환하러
④ 돈을 합쳐서 엄마 선물을 같이 사기 위해서

11 다음을 듣고, 무엇에 관한 설명인지 고르시오.

①   ②

③   ④

12 대화를 듣고, 여자가 남자에게 전화를 건 목적을 고르시오.

① 소지를 변경하려고
② TV 위성을 고치려고
③ TV를 배달해 달라고
④ 주 위성방송을 설치하려고

13 대화를 듣고, 엄마가 없을 때 남자가 할 수 없는 일을 고르시오.

① 책 읽기
② 간식 먹기
③ TV 보기
④ 나가서 농구 하기

14 대화를 듣고, 남자의 마지막 말의 의도로 알맞은 것을 고르시오.

① 사과 ② 후회
③ 거절 ④ 승낙

15 대화를 듣고, 여자가 공항에 도착할 시각으로 알맞은 것을 고르시오.

① 1:15 ② 2:30
③ 2:45 ④ 3:00

16 대화를 듣고, 남자의 심경으로 가장 알맞은 것을 고르시오.

① proud
② nervous
③ tired
④ disappointed

17 다음을 듣고, 상황과 어울리는 속담을 고르시오.

① Walls have ears.
② Seeing is believing.
③ Look before you leap.
④ No news is good news.

18 다음을 듣고, 각 요일별 날씨가 바르게 연결된 것을 고르시오

① 수요일 - 흐린
② 목요일 - 비가 오는
③ 금요일 - 따뜻한
④ 토요일 - 화창한

[19~20] 대화를 듣고, 남자의 마지막 말에 이어질 여자의 응답으로 가장 적절한 것을 고르시오.

19

① 3281 West 5th St.
② Would you tell me John's number?
③ 987-4563.
④ Seven is my favorite number.

20

① The blue one is much nicer.
② I don't know what to say.
③ I bought the jacket yesterday.
④ Here. Let me take it.

1 다음을 듣고, 그림의 상황에 가장 알맞은 대화를 고르시오.

① ② ③ ④

① W _____ _____ do you want to buy?

M What about these chocolate chip ones?

② W Help yourself to some cookies. _____ _____ _____ today.

M Thanks, Mom. You're a great baker.

③ W Dinner will _____ _____ _____.

M Great. I'm very hungry.

④ W John, you eat too many snacks. _____ _____ _____.

M OK, Mom. I won't eat anymore snacks.

2 다음을 듣고, 무엇에 관한 내용인지 고르시오.

① takeoff
② landing
③ boarding
④ seat belt

M Passengers can now board Flight AC 456. Passengers will board the plane _____ _____. People sitting at the back of the plane will _____ _____ _____. People who _____ _____ _____ _____ 45 to 55 can now get on the plane. Please have your ticket and _____ _____ _____.

3 대화를 듣고, 대화 직후 여자가 할 일을 고르시오.

① 쇼핑하기
② 집으로 가기
③ 사진관에서 기다리기
④ 커피숍에서 기다리기

M Good afternoon. How may I help you?

W Would you _____ _____ _____, please?

M OK. Your photos will be in 30 minutes.

W 30 minutes? _____ _____.

M Yes.

W Hmm... I was going to go home. But _____ _____ _____ _____.

M You can go have coffee in the coffee shop.

W No, _____ _____ _____ _____ in the mall. I like shopping more than drinking coffee.

4 대화를 듣고, 내용과 일치하지 <u>않는</u> 것을 고르시오.

① 할아버지 댁은 여자네 집에서 가깝다.
② 할머니는 음식을 여자에게 갖다 주신다.
③ 할머니는 음식을 많이 만드신다.
④ 여자는 할아버지와 할머니를 한 달에 서너 번 만난다.

M Where do your grandparents live?
W They live a few minutes away from us.
M So you _____ _____ _____ _____ .
W Yes, I guess so. I see them three or _____ _____ _____ _____ . I love them.
M Oh, that's nice.
W In addition, grandmother cooks a lot of food and _____ _____ _____ for us to eat.

5 대화를 듣고, 여자가 남자에게 읽기를 바라는 뉴스를 고르시오.

① 국내면
② 정치면
③ 국제면
④ 스포츠면

M May I have _____ _____ _____ ?
W You only read the sports section of the newspaper.
M I sometimes read _____ _____ _____ , too.
W You should read the international news, too. I always read _____ _____ _____ _____ . You can learn a lot about the world from this section.
M OK. I'll read it when you're done.

6 대화를 듣고, 두 사람이 현재 있는 장소를 고르시오.

① art museum
② concert hall
③ library
④ photograph shop

M _____ _____ is very beautiful.
W Yes, it is. Let's see. It says here that _____ _____ _____ in 1889.
M Really?
W Yes, it's one of his most famous paintings. I like it very much.
M He is your favorite painter.
W That's right. That's why I really wanted to come to _____ _____ .
M Yes, these paintings will _____ _____ _____ for two weeks.

7 다음을 듣고, 두 사람의 대화가 <u>어색한</u> 것을 고르시오.

①   ②   ③   ④

① **M** Do you know _____ _____ _____ _____ ?
   W Yes, I do. We went to _____ _____ _____ _____ together.
② **M** I don't feel well.
   W You should go home and get some rest.
③ **M** Can you help me, please?
   W Nice to hear that. _____ _____ _____ _____ .
④ **M** How do you usually come to school?
   W _____ _____ _____ _____ with my younger sister.

8 다음을 듣고, 내용에 가장 알맞은 안내문을 고르시오.

① DON'T TOUCH THE ANIMALS
② BE CAREFUL OF WILD ANIMALS
③ FASTEN YOUR SEAT BELT
④ DON'T GIVE FOOD TO THE ANIMALS

M Welcome to Safari Zoo Park's train ride. Please sit down. The train _____ _____ _____. The train will travel _____ _____ _____. It will take 45 minutes. You will get close to some lions and tigers. Please _____ _____ _____ _____ to any of the animals. You may _____ _____ _____ _____ when it stops at the end.

9 대화를 듣고, 여자의 직업으로 알맞은 것을 고르시오.

① cook
② cashier
③ waitress
④ housewife

M _____ _____ _____ _____?
W Yes, when the restaurant is busy, we must work very hard.
M It must be very hot in the kitchen.
W It is. But I like to make food. I have _____ _____ _____ for my food. I'm glad to see people happy with it.
M Well, I will come to the restaurant to _____ _____ _____ next week.
W Good. See you then.

10 대화를 듣고, 두 사람이 쇼핑하러 가는 이유를 고르시오.

① 엄마의 생신 선물을 교환하러
② 각자 엄마의 생신 선물을 사기 위해서
③ 엄마에게 받은 책 생일 선물을 교환하러
④ 돈을 합쳐서 엄마 선물을 같이 사기 위해서

M Where are you going?
W I'm going shopping.
M Shopping again! You went shopping with your friend last week.
W I'm shopping for a birthday present for my mom. Her birthday is _____ _____ _____ _____.
M Oh, I haven't got her a present yet.
W _____ _____ _____. We can each buy a present for my mom. I think I'll give her _____ _____ _____. How about you?

11 다음을 듣고, 무엇에 관한 설명인지 고르시오.

① ② ③ ④

M Almost every office, school and business has one of these. It makes lots of _____ _____ _____ as well as papers. You open the cover, _____ _____ _____ to be copied face-down, close the cover and _____ _____ _____. Then a copy comes out of the side of this.

12 대화를 듣고, 여자가 남자에게 전화를 건 목적을 고르시오.

① 소지를 변경하려고
② TV 위성을 고치려고
③ TV를 배달해 달라고
④ 주 위성방송을 설치하려고

[Telephone rings.]

M Hello. World Satellite TV.

W Hello. I have a problem. Some TV channels are not clear. I can't watch _____ _____.

M I will send a repairperson to your house this afternoon.

W Thank you. I live at 874 Pine Street, apartment 10.

M _____ _____ _____ _____ at 2?

W Yes.

M OK. _____ _____ will be there at 2.

13 대화를 듣고, 엄마가 없을 때 남자가 할 수 없는 일을 고르시오.

① 책 읽기
② 간식 먹기
③ TV 보기
④ 나가서 농구 하기

W I'm leaving now, David. See you around 9 p.m.

M OK. Say hi to aunt Gloria and everyone for me.

W I will do that. Now remember _____ _____ _____ _____.

M Yes, _____ _____.

W Go outside and play basketball. Get some exercise. You watch too much TV.

M I played soccer after school, Mom. _____ _____ _____.

W And have some snacks _____ _____ _____ _____ _____ when you are hungry.

M Yes, I will. Don't worry, Mom

14 대화를 듣고, 남자의 마지막 말의 의도로 알맞은 것을 고르시오.

① 사과
② 후회
③ 거절
④ 승낙

M Your food _____ _____.

W It is very good. Do you want to eat some?

M Yes, thanks. [pause] Oh, it's good. Your spaghetti is _____ _____ _____ _____ _____.

W I'll give you _____ _____ _____ _____.

M Thanks. Next time I will order the spaghetti.

15 대화를 듣고, 여자가 공항에 도착할 시각으로 알맞은 것을 고르시오.

① 1:15
② 2:30
③ 2:45
④ 3:00

M You have to be at the airport around 3 o'clock, right?

W Yes, I do.

M Will you take a subway or bus?

W I want to take a bus. _____ _____ _____ _____.

M Well, there are two airport buses you can take.

W _____ _____ _____ _____?

M 1:10 and 1:30. The trips take _____ _____ _____

_____ _____.

W I'll take the bus that leaves at 1:30.

16 대화를 듣고, 남자의 심경으로 가장 알맞은 것을 고르시오.

① proud
② nervous
③ tired
④ disappointed

M You said you would be home at 9 p.m.

W Yes, I promised that this morning.

M But it's 10:30 and you just got home.

W I'm so sorry, Dad. _____ _____ _____ had to prepare our presentation for the next English class.

M But you must _____ _____ _____. I must be able to trust you.

W I won't _____ _____ _____ _____.

17 다음을 듣고, 상황과 어울리는 속담을 고르시오.

① Walls have ears.
② Seeing is believing.
③ Look before you leap.
④ No news is good news.

M There is a hurricane. Many buildings _____ _____. Your house _____ _____. The telephone doesn't work. But your family members in another city are worried about you. If they _____ _____ _____ _____, they might say this famous English phrase so that _____ _____ _____.

18 다음을 듣고, 각 요일별 날씨가 바르게 연결된 것을 고르시오

① 수요일 – 흐린
② 목요일 – 비가 오는
③ 금요일 – 따뜻한
④ 토요일 – 화창한

M This is the weather report for Wednesday. It's going to _____ _____ _____ _____ today. The rain showers will continue for three days. Then on Saturday it will be cloudy and warm. You can still enjoy outdoor activities _____ _____ _____ _____ _____. Remember to bring an umbrella to work _____ _____ _____ _____.

19 대화를 듣고, 남자의 마지막 말에 이어질 여자의 응답으로 가장 적절한 것을 고르시오.

① 3281 West 5th St.
② Would you tell me John's number?
③ 987-4563.
④ Seven is my favorite number.

[Telephone rings.]
M Hello.
W Hello, is John at home?
M John? There is no one here _____ _____ _____.
W Isn't this _____ _____ _____?
M No, it isn't. What number do you _____ _____ _____?
W _____

20 대화를 듣고, 남자의 마지막 말에 이어질 여자의 응답으로 가장 적절한 것을 고르시오.

① The blue one is much nicer.
② I don't know what to say.
③ I bought the jacket yesterday.
④ Here. Let me take it.

W Hello, Peter.
M Hi, Mary. I'm sorry I'm late.
W That's alright.
M _____ _____ _____ in traffic. It took almost 2 hours to get here.
W That's too bad. But I'm glad _____ _____ _____ _____. We were all waiting for you.
M _____ _____ _____ put my jacket?
W _____

A Write down the definition of each word or phrase.

1	develop	11	vote
2	director	12	medicine
3	bother	13	passenger
4	avoid	14	row
5	exchange	15	fasten
6	traffic	16	prepare
7	expire	17	destroy
8	validity	18	household
9	deposit	19	consider
10	carry	20	continent

B Match each word with the right definition.

1	satellite		a	사막
2	exhibit		b	사적인, 개인적인
3	private		c	손해[피해]를 입은
4	continue		d	마중 나가다, 태우러 가다
5	solve		e	어린 시절, 유년시대
6	flight		f	명예, 영광
7	damaged		g	풀다, 해결하다
8	happen		h	비행, 항공편
9	honor		i	전시(하다), 전람(하다)
10	get off		j	도처에, 구석구석까지
11	phrase		k	~에서 내리다
12	desert		l	위성, 위성방송
13	pick up		m	일어나다, 벌어지다
14	throughout		n	구, 숙어, 관용구
15	childhood		o	계속되다, 지속되다

C Choose the best answer for the blank.

1 We make many things _____ paper.

    a. with   b. by   c. out of

2 Let's _____ to a movie.

    a. not go   b. don't go   c. go not

3 Can you _____ a copy of it for me?

    a. hold   c. do   c. make

4 Actually we have three people who go _____ the name of James.

    a. with   b. by   c. on

5 She is _____ taller than I thought.

    a. much   b. very   c. more

6 I saw him as _____ as his sister.

    a. good   b. well   c. much

D Complete the short dialogues.

1 A: I'm broke this month.

    B: Don't worry about it. It's my _____.

2 A: Mother's birthday is just around the _____.

    B: Let's buy a present for her tomorrow.

3 A: It took almost 2 hours to get here.

    B: That's too bad. But I'm glad you finally made _____.

4 A: Let's go there by bus now.

    B: I don't want to be _____ in a traffic jam.

5 A: I'll miss you so much.

    B: Me too. I'll call you _____ my arrival.

1 다음을 듣고, 무엇에 관한 설명인지 고르시오.

①

②

③

④

2 다음을 듣고, 상미에 관해 알 수 <u>없는</u> 것을 고르시오.

① 어디서 지내고 있는지
② 무엇을 하고 있는지
③ 언제 집으로 돌아가는지
④ 무엇을 먹고 싶어 하는지

3 대화를 듣고, 내용과 일치하지 <u>않는</u> 것을 고르시오.

① 여자는 꽃을 살 것이다.
② 남자는 주스를 살 것이다.
③ 남자는 병문안 갈 것이다.
④ 남자의 친구는 병원에 입원했다.

4 다음을 듣고, 오늘의 날씨로 예상되는 것을 고르시오.

① rainy
② windy
③ sunny
④ cloudy

5 대화를 듣고, 여자의 직업으로 알맞은 것을 고르시오.

① vet
② zoo keeper
③ park ranger
④ pet store shopkeeper

6 대화를 듣고, 여자가 마지막에 한 말의 의도를 고르시오.

① 칭찬
② 홍보
③ 충고
④ 경고

7 대화를 듣고, 상황에 알맞은 표지판을 고르시오.

①   ②

③   ④

8 대화를 듣고, 두 사람이 부모님께 드린 것이 <u>아닌</u> 것을 고르시오.

① 돈
② 모자
③ 저녁식사
④ 넥타이

9 대화를 듣고, 두 사람이 서점에 가는 이유를 고르시오.

① 책을 사러
② 친구를 만나러
③ 티켓을 예매하러
④ 시간을 때우러

10 대화를 듣고, 여자가 집에 도착할 시각을 고르시오.

① 11:05
② 11:15
③ 12:00
④ 12:15

11 다음을 듣고, 식당 광고문의 내용과 일치하지 <u>않는</u> 것을 고르시오.

Seafood Garden Restaurant
345 West 3rd St
Tel: 02-2987-4934

A wonderful seafood buffet at a cheap price!
- $20 adults   - $13 children
※ Open for lunch and dinner.
※ Closed on Mondays.
※ Reservations not necessary.

①   ②   ③   ④

12 다음을 듣고, 두 사람의 대화가 <u>어색한</u> 것을 고르시오.

①   ②   ③   ④

13 대화를 듣고, 남자가 지불해야 될 금액을 고르시오.

① $35
② $60
③ $70
④ $120

14 대화를 듣고, 대화가 이루어지는 장소를 고르시오.

① hospital
② airport
③ hotel
④ fitness club

15 대화를 듣고, 두 사람이 지금 함께 할 일을 고르시오.

① 수영하기
② 배구하기
③ 바닷가 가기
④ 휴식을 취하기

16 대화를 듣고, 여자의 증상이 <u>아닌</u> 것을 고르시오.

① 두통
② 복통
③ 눈의 피로
④ 어깨 결림

17 다음을 듣고, 그림의 상황에 가장 알맞은 대화를 고르시오.

①   ②   ③   ④

18 대화를 듣고, 남자의 심경으로 가장 알맞은 것을 고르시오.

① excited
② bored
③ frustrated
④ worried

[19~20] 대화를 듣고, 마지막 말에 이어질 응답으로 가장 적절한 것을 고르시오.

19

① What is your name?
② Does she know you?
③ Can you meet her at 8?
④ Where do you want to meet?

20

① It's my pleasure.
② That's good news.
③ Happy to meet you again.
④ Sally, this is my friend.

1 다음을 듣고, 무엇에 관한 설명인지 고르시오.

① (headphones) ② (microphone)
③ (speaker) ④ (USB drive)

M Most people _____ _____ _____ _____ to music on their MP3 player. You plug these into your MP3 player. You can use these to listen to TV shows or movies on a computer or _____ _____ _____, too. Most of the time these _____ _____ _____ _____. They cover your ears. Sound comes out of them into your ears.

2 다음을 듣고, 상미에 관해 알 수 없는 것을 고르시오.

① 어디서 지내고 있는지
② 무엇을 하고 있는지
③ 언제 집으로 돌아가는지
④ 무엇을 먹고 싶어 하는지

W Sangmi _____ _____ _____. She is traveling in Europe _____ _____ _____. It is fun but hard. She is lonely sometimes. And she wants to eat her mother's cooking. These days _____ _____ _____ _____. It is not always comfortable. She wants to feel comfortable at home.

3 대화를 듣고, 내용과 일치하지 않는 것을 고르시오.

① 여자는 꽃을 살 것이다.
② 남자는 주스를 살 것이다.
③ 남자는 병문안 갈 것이다.
④ 남자의 친구는 병원에 입원했다.

M I have to _____ _____ _____ _____ this afternoon.
W Why is that? Are you sick?
M No. My friend is sick. I have to visit my friend. He _____ _____ _____ on his right leg yesterday.
W Oh, that's nice of you. Make sure to bring him some flowers.
M He doesn't like flowers. I will _____ _____ _____ _____.

4 다음을 듣고, 오늘의 날씨로 예상되는 것을 고르시오.

① rainy
② windy
③ sunny
④ cloudy

W Good morning. This is the weather forecast. Today will be cloudy with _____ _____ _____ _____. The clouds will _____ _____ _____, so the weather will be sunny. So you can look forward to a beautiful day tomorrow.

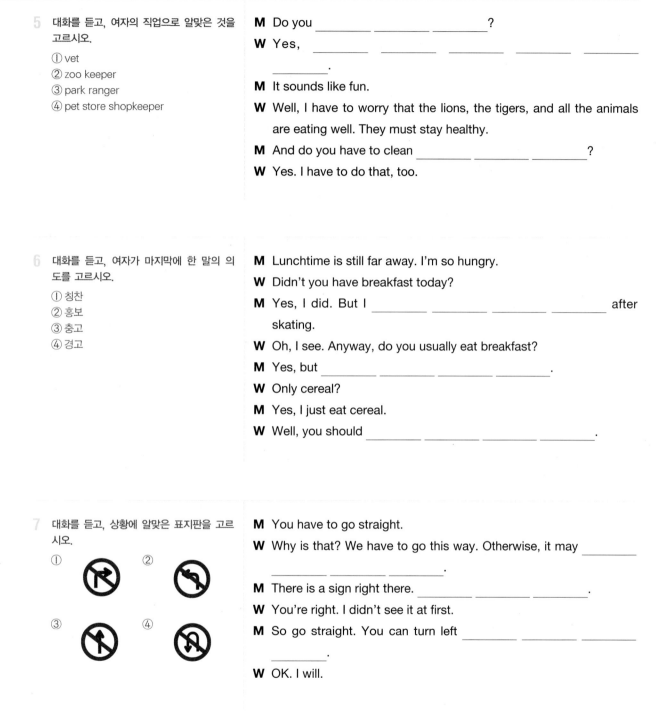

5 대화를 듣고, 여자의 직업으로 알맞은 것을 고르시오.

① vet
② zoo keeper
③ park ranger
④ pet store shopkeeper

M Do you _____ _____ _____?

W Yes, _____ _____ _____ _____ _____
_____ .

M It sounds like fun.

W Well, I have to worry that the lions, the tigers, and all the animals are eating well. They must stay healthy.

M And do you have to clean _____ _____ _____?

W Yes. I have to do that, too.

6 대화를 듣고, 여자가 마지막에 한 말의 의도를 고르시오.

① 칭찬
② 홍보
③ 충고
④ 경고

M Lunchtime is still far away. I'm so hungry.

W Didn't you have breakfast today?

M Yes, I did. But I _____ _____ _____ _____ after skating.

W Oh, I see. Anyway, do you usually eat breakfast?

M Yes, but _____ _____ _____ _____ .

W Only cereal?

M Yes, I just eat cereal.

W Well, you should _____ _____ _____ _____ .

7 대화를 듣고, 상황에 알맞은 표지판을 고르시오.

① ② ③ ④

M You have to go straight.

W Why is that? We have to go this way. Otherwise, it may _____
_____ _____ _____ .

M There is a sign right there. _____ _____ _____ .

W You're right. I didn't see it at first.

M So go straight. You can turn left _____ _____ _____
_____ .

W OK. I will.

8 대화를 듣고, 두 사람이 부모님께 드린 것이 <u>아닌</u> 것을 고르시오.

① 돈
② 모자
③ 저녁식사
④ 넥타이

M Did you get some flowers for your mom and dad?

W No, I didn't.

M What did you buy them _____ _____ _____?

W I bought my mom a hat and _____ _____ _____ _____.

M I cooked dinner for my parents.

W You didn't have money, so you couldn't _____ _____ _____ for their presents. But I _____ _____ _____ for their presents.

9 대화를 듣고, 두 사람이 서점에 가는 이유를 고르시오.

① 책을 사러
② 친구를 만나러
③ 티켓을 예매하러
④ 시간을 때우러

M Let's eat some snacks before the show starts.

W It starts in 30 minutes. _____ _____ _____ _____.

M How about a burger and fries? It won't take a long time.

W No, I want something else.

M OK. We'll eat something special _____ _____ _____. Let's go to the bookstore for 15 or 20 minutes.

W OK. There are always lots of things _____ _____ _____.

10 대화를 듣고, 여자가 집에 도착할 시각을 고르시오.

① 11:05
② 11:15
③ 12:00
④ 12:15

M How long does it take you to go home from here?

W _____ _____ _____. I have to take a subway.

M What time is _____ _____ _____?

W 11:15. If I miss the 11:15, I have to take a taxi and it's expensive.

M Well, you _____ _____ _____ to the subway station. It's 11:05. I can come with you to the station.

11 다음을 듣고, 식당 광고문의 내용과 일치하지 <u>않는</u> 것을 고르시오.

Seafood Garden Restaurant
345 West 3rd St
Tel: 02-2987-4934

A wonderful seafood buffet at a cheap price!
- $20 adults   - $13 children
※ Open for lunch and dinner.
※ Closed on Mondays.
※ Reservations not necessary.

① ② ③ ④

W ① Seafood Garden Restaurant is _____ _____ _____.
② The restaurant is _____ _____ _____.
③ People _____ _____ _____ _____ a reservation.
④ The restaurant is open for lunch and dinner.

12 다음을 듣고, 두 사람의 대화가 <u>어색한</u> 것을 고르시오.

① ② ③ ④

① M Would you tell me why you like him?
W He is very humorous, so he _____ _____ _____.
② M Are you busy?
W Well, I have many things to do now.
③ M How about next week?
W OK. Let's meet next Monday.
④ M What do you _____ _____ _____ _____?
W I don't feel well right now.

13 대화를 듣고, 남자가 지불해야 될 금액을 고르시오.
① $35
② $60
③ $70
④ $120

W Hello. How may I help you?
M How much is a bus ticket to Longtown?
W _____.
M Is that round trip or one way?
W One way. _____ _____ _____ ticket is $60.
M I need _____ _____ _____, please. When will the next bus leave for Longtown?
W The next bus will leave in 10 minutes.

14 대화를 듣고, 대화가 이루어지는 장소를 고르시오.

① hospital
② airport
③ hotel
④ fitness club

M I had a reservation a week ago.

W What is your name, sir?

M John Smith.

W Let me see. Yes, here is your reservation. You _____ _____ _____ _____ for three nights.

M Yes, that is correct. How much _____ _____ _____ _____ ?

W It's $120 a night.

M By the way, is there a hospital near here? _____ _____ _____ _____ .

15 대화를 듣고, 두 사람이 지금 함께 할 일을 고르시오.

① 수영하기
② 배구하기
③ 바닷가 가기
④ 휴식을 취하기

M It's a beautiful sunny day.

W We picked a great day to come to the beach.

M Let's go swimming.

W No, let's _____ _____ _____ .

M Yes, that's a better idea. After I get hot playing volleyball, I can _____ _____ _____ _____ _____ .

W I'll _____ _____ _____ .

M Great. Let's go.

16 대화를 듣고, 여자의 증상이 <u>아닌</u> 것을 고르시오.

① 두통
② 복통
③ 눈의 피로
④ 어깨 결림

M Good morning. You look tired.

W Yes, I _____ _____ _____ because of my exams. My eyes and head hurt from reading for so long.

M Do you need new glasses?

W No, I don't think so, Dad. _____ _____ _____ _____ , too.

M Do you need some medicine?

W I think I'm just worried about tomorrow's tests.

M If you are doing your best, you won't have to _____ _____ _____ .

17 다음을 듣고, 그림의 상황에 가장 알맞은 대화를 고르시오.

① ② ③ ④

① **M** Who is this guy _____ _____ _____ ?
   W He is my favorite singer.

② **M** _____ _____ this doll is!
   W Right. It was a birthday present my friend gave me.

③ **M** _____ _____ _____ _____ in the picture?
   W She is an Australian friend who I met last summer.

④ **M** Have you finished your English homework?
   W Yes. I finished it _____ _____ _____ .

18 대화를 듣고, 남자의 심경으로 가장 알맞은 것을 고르시오.

① excited
② bored
③ frustrated
④ worried

M I can't _____ _____ _____ that goes right there.
W I am sure it is here. Did you look carefully?
M Yes, I did. Doing puzzles is stressful sometimes.
W _____ _____ _____ _____ .
M But I've tried to find the piece that goes there, but I can't find it. I don't want to _____ _____ _____ _____ .
W Come on, look for that piece carefully.

19 대화를 듣고, 마지막 말에 이어질 응답으로 가장 적절한 것을 고르시오.

① What is your name?
② Does she know you?
③ Can you meet her at 8?
④ Where do you want to meet?

[Telephone rings.]
M Hello.
W Hello, is Susan there? I'm Susan's classmate.
M No, I'm afraid _____ _____ _____ right now.
W Oh, when will she be home?
M At about 8 p.m. She went to buy some books with her dad.
W Can you _____ _____ _____ _____ me, please?
M Sure. _____

20 대화를 듣고, 마지막 말에 이어질 응답으로 가장 적절한 것을 고르시오.

① It's my pleasure.
② That's good news.
③ Happy to meet you again.
④ Sally, this is my friend.

M It's _____ _____ _____ , Jennifer.
W Thank you. Did you have some pizza?
M Yes, I had some pizza. You have some nice friends.
W That's right. Did you talk to Sally? I think you two can _____ _____ _____ .
M Yes, I did. She is very nice. _____ _____ _____ , I want to thank you for inviting me.
W _____

1 다음을 듣고, 그림을 가장 적절하게 묘사한 것을 고르시오.

①   ②   ③   ④

2 다음을 듣고, 요일별 날씨로 바르지 <u>않은</u> 것을 고르시오.

① 오늘 – cool
② 오늘 – cloudy
③ 내일 – windy
④ 내일 – warm

3 대화를 듣고, 대화가 이루어지는 장소를 고르시오.

① shoe store
② dry cleaner's
③ clothing shop
④ changing room

4 대화를 듣고, 현장학습에서 한 일이 <u>아닌</u> 것을 고르시오.

① 박물관 가기
② 등산하기
③ 카드게임 하기
④ 노래 부르기

5 다음을 듣고, 무엇에 관한 안내인지 고르시오.

① 어휘력 향상법
② 기억력 향상법
③ 영어 책을 읽는 요령
④ 영어 성적 올리는 방법

6 대화를 듣고, 남자의 장래희망으로 알맞은 것을 고르시오.

① tour guide
② traveler
③ travel agent
④ flight attendant

7 다음을 듣고, 두 사람의 대화가 <u>어색한</u> 것을 고르시오.

①   ②   ③   ④

8 대화를 듣고, 여자가 남자에게 전화를 건 목적을 고르시오.

① 공부하라고
② 집에 오라고
③ 저녁식사에 초대하려고
④ 과학 과제를 같이 하자고

9 다음을 듣고, 상황에 알맞은 속담을 고르시오.

① Birds of a feather flock together.
② The pot calls the kettle black.
③ Too many cooks spoil the broth.
④ A bad workman blames his tools.

10 다음을 듣고, 숙제를 잊지 않고 하기 위해서 남자가 하는 일로 알맞은 것을 고르시오.

① 친구에게 물어본다.
② 휴대폰에 입력한다.
③ 숙제공책에 기록한다.
④ 손바닥에 적어둔다.

11 대화를 듣고, 여자의 증상으로 알맞은 것을 고르시오.

①   ②

③ ④

12 다음을 듣고, Betty와 John이 방문했던 나라로 언급되지 <u>않은</u> 것을 고르시오.
① 영국　　　　　　② 독일
③ 스페인　　　　　④ 포르투갈

13 다음을 듣고, 주어진 상황에서 할 수 있는 말로 가장 적절한 것을 고르시오.
① You know I did my best.
② Good luck in the game.
③ Cheer up! You played well.
④ You should have won the game.

14 다음을 듣고, 표의 내용과 일치하지 <u>않는</u> 것을 고르시오.

Name	Time to go to bed	Time to get up
Inho	10:00	7:00
Sangmin	10:00	7:30
Jihyun	10:30	7:20

① ② ③ ④

15 대화를 듣고, 남자의 편지가 도착하는 데 걸리는 날 수를 고르시오.
① 1일　　② 2일　　③ 3일　　④ 4일

16 대화를 듣고, 여자가 하는 말의 의도로 알맞은 것을 고르시오.
① 소개　　② 변명　　③ 충고　　④ 부탁

17 다음을 듣고, 도표의 내용과 일치하지 <u>않는</u> 것을 고르시오.

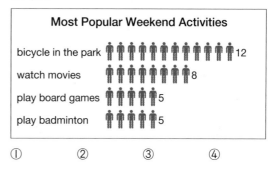

① ② ③ ④

18 대화를 듣고, 남자의 기분으로 가장 알맞은 것을 고르시오.
① proud
② scared
③ surprised
④ disappointed

[19-20] 대화를 듣고, 여자의 마지막 말에 이어질 남자의 응답으로 가장 적절한 것을 고르시오.

19
① Please speak slowly.
② That's very kind of you.
③ Could you lend me a notebook?
④ That's all right. You have only one.

20
① Yes. Could you close it for me?
② No. You can leave it open.
③ Yes. Give me my sweater, please.
④ No, it's OK. Turn down the heat.

1 다음을 듣고, 그림을 가장 적절하게 묘사한
  것을 고르시오.

  ① ② ③ ④

W ① _____ _____ _____ _____ a customer in a
    shop.
  ② A woman is paying for groceries.
  ③ The older woman is ordering food _____ _____
    _____ _____.
  ④ The man and woman are shopping for groceries.

2 다음을 듣고, 요일별 날씨로 바르지 <u>않은</u>
  것을 고르시오.
  ① 오늘 – cool
  ② 오늘 – cloudy
  ③ 내일 – windy
  ④ 내일 – warm

M Good evening, ABS listeners. I'm Mark Mathers with the 6 o'clock
  weather report. It was _____ _____ _____ today.
  Tomorrow it will be cloudy again. But it will also be windy
  tomorrow. The sun will _____ _____ _____ _____.
  Tomorrow will be a good day to _____ _____ _____.

3 대화를 듣고, 대화가 이루어지는 장소를 고
  르시오.
  ① shoe store
  ② dry cleaner's
  ③ clothing shop
  ④ changing room

W What size do you need, sir?
M I need an 84 cm waist.
W OK. Here is _____ _____ _____ _____ in that size.
M Where is the changing room?
W _____ _____, sir.
M OK. I will go and _____ _____ _____.

4 대화를 듣고, 현장학습에서 한 일이 <u>아닌</u>
  것을 고르시오.
  ① 박물관 가기
  ② 등산하기
  ③ 카드게임 하기
  ④ 노래 부르기

M The school field trip was terrible because of the rain.
W Did you _____ _____ _____ _____?
M No, we didn't. We waited on the bus for _____ _____
  _____ _____. But it didn't.
W What did you do _____ _____ _____?
M Singing, playing cards and _____ _____ _____
  _____. After a few hours, we visited a museum.

5 다음을 듣고, 무엇에 관한 안내인지 고르시오.

① 어휘력 향상법
② 기억력 향상법
③ 영어 책을 읽는 요령
④ 영어 성적 올리는 방법

M Do you want to improve your English vocabulary? I think you should read a lot to _____ _____ _____. When you read a word a few times _____ _____ _____, you can remember it easily. You learn the word _____ _____ _____ to remember it. So read lots of books.

---

6 대화를 듣고, 남자의 장래희망으로 알맞은 것을 고르시오.

① tour guide
② traveler
③ travel agent
④ flight attendant

M I want to travel all over the world.

W Do you like to live in foreign countries?

M Not really. But I do like to meet new people. So I want to _____ _____ _____.

W I see. You can go everywhere _____ _____.

M That's right. I will travel outside of Korea to _____ _____ _____ from different cultures all over the world.

---

7 다음을 듣고, 두 사람의 대화가 <u>어색한</u> 것을 고르시오.

①   ②   ③   ④

① **W** Thank you very much for your help.
   M _____ _____. _____.

② **W** How old is your sister?
   M She was born on September 15th.

③ **W** Is there _____ _____ _____?
   M Yes, there is. But not much.

④ **W** There is a test tomorrow. The music is too loud.
   M Ah, I'm sorry. I will _____ _____ _____.

---

8 대화를 듣고, 여자가 남자에게 전화를 건 목적을 고르시오.

① 공부하라고
② 집에 오라고
③ 저녁식사에 초대하려고
④ 과학 과제를 같이 하자고

[Cell phone rings.]

M Hello.

W Hello, Mike. This is Mom.

M Oh, hi, Mom.

W I told you to come home at 7 for dinner.

M I'm sorry, Mom. Peter and I were busy _____ _____ _____ _____ our science project. We have to hand it in this Friday.

W Well, now hurry home. You must be hungry.

M I am. _____ _____ in 10 minutes.

9 다음을 듣고, 상황에 알맞은 속담을 고르시오.

① Birds of a feather flock together.
② The pot calls the kettle black.
③ Too many cooks spoil the broth.
④ A bad workman blames his tools.

W My classroom has _____ _____ _____. There are the boys who like to play sports and the girls who love pop music. And the boys _____ _____ _____ _____ usually love computer games. All they do is talking about computer games. The people _____ _____ _____ _____ talk to people _____ _____ _____ _____.

10 다음을 듣고, 숙제를 잊지 않고 하기 위해서 남자가 하는 일로 알맞은 것을 고르시오.

① 친구에게 물어본다.
② 핸드폰에 입력한다.
③ 숙제공책에 기록한다.
④ 손바닥에 적어둔다.

M Paul writes down his homework _____ _____ _____ _____. He calls it his homework notebook. When he goes home, he looks at the notebook. The homework for each subject _____ _____ _____. He never forgets to do his homework. So his friends often call him _____ _____ _____ _____.

11 대화를 듣고, 여자의 증상으로 알맞은 것을 고르시오.

① ② ③ ④

M _____ _____ _____. What's wrong? Are you sick?
W Yes, I don't feel well.
M Do you have a cold? Many people around us _____ _____ _____ these days.
W No, I think it's just _____ _____ _____.
M What is that? Is there something wrong with you?
W Well, I have been reading and studying all day.
M Go get some rest.

12 다음을 듣고, Betty와 John이 방문했던 나라로 언급되지 <u>않은</u> 것을 고르시오.

① 영국
② 독일
③ 스페인
④ 포르투갈

W Betty and John _____ _____ _____ last year. They stopped working. Now they _____ _____ _____ _____. They have been to Europe many times. Last summer they went to Britain and Scotland. _____ _____ _____ they visited Spain and Portugal. Now in wintertime _____ _____ _____ _____ to Germany and Greece.

13 다음을 듣고, 주어진 상황에서 할 수 있는 말로 가장 적절한 것을 고르시오.

① You know I did my best.
② Good luck in the game.
③ Cheer up! You played well.
④ You should have won the game.

M Your friend is really sad because his soccer team _____ _____ _____ _____. He played well. But his team lost. The score was 1-0. _____ _____ _____. You want to _____ _____ _____ _____. What would you say to your friend?

14 다음을 듣고, 표의 내용과 일치하지 <u>않는</u> 것을 고르시오.

Name	Time to go to bed	Time to get up
Inho	10:00	7:00
Sangmin	10:00	7:30
Jihyun	10:30	7:20

① ② ③ ④

W ① Inho sleeps for 9 hours _____ _____.
② Sangmin gets up _____ _____.
③ Jihyun gets up earlier than Inho does.
④ Sangmin goes to bed _____ _____ _____ as Inho.

15 대화를 듣고, 남자의 편지가 도착하는 데 걸리는 날수를 고르시오.

① 1일
② 2일
③ 3일
④ 4일

M How many days will it take for this letter to arrive?

W It will take 4 days _____ _____ _____. But if you send it by registered mail, it will _____ _____ _____.

M I want it to arrive tomorrow.

W We do have _____ _____ _____. But it is expensive. It will cost $15.

M It's too expensive. I will send it _____ _____ _____.

16 대화를 듣고, 여자가 하는 말의 의도로 알맞은 것을 고르시오.

① 소개
② 변명
③ 충고
④ 부탁

M I'm home.

W You came home _____ _____ _____. I'm sorry dinner isn't ready, honey.

M That's OK. I'll wait.

W I was cooking, _____ _____ _____ _____ and my sister wanted to talk.

M And you talked and talked.

W Yes, she had _____ _____ _____.

17 다음을 듣고, 도표의 내용과 일치하지 <u>않는</u> 것을 고르시오.

Most Popular Weekend Activities	
bicycle in the park	🚶🚶🚶🚶🚶🚶🚶🚶🚶🚶🚶🚶 12
watch movies	🚶🚶🚶🚶🚶🚶🚶🚶 8
play board games	🚶🚶🚶🚶🚶 5
play badminton	🚶🚶🚶🚶🚶 5

① ② ③ ④

M ① Bicycling in the park is _____ _____ _____ _____.

② Watching movies is not as popular as bicycling.

③ Five students like to _____ _____ _____ with their friends.

④ Playing board games is _____ _____ _____ playing badminton.

18 대화를 듣고, 남자의 기분으로 가장 알맞은 것을 고르시오.

① proud
② scared
③ surprised
④ disappointed

M Jimin, you did really well.

W But I didn't win the singing contest. I'm so sad.

M Winning isn't the most important thing. _____ _____ _____ _____.

W Thanks, Dad. That means a lot to me. I'll remember your words and _____ _____ _____.

M I am really happy that you're such a nice, _____ _____.

19 대화를 듣고, 여자의 마지막 말에 이어질 남자의 응답으로 가장 적절한 것을 고르시오.

① Please speak slowly.
② That's very kind of you.
③ Could you lend me a notebook?
④ That's all right. You have only one.

W Why aren't you writing down what the teacher said? What the teacher said today _____ _____ _____ for the test.

M _____ _____ _____ my pencil.

W Did you lose your pencil case?

M Yes, I guess so. I couldn't find it after lunch.

W I will _____ _____ _____ _____.

M _____

20 대화를 듣고, 여자의 마지막 말에 이어질 남자의 응답으로 가장 적절한 것을 고르시오.

① Yes. Could you close it for me?
② No. You can leave it open.
③ Yes. Give me my sweater, please.
④ No, it's OK. Turn down the heat.

M I'm very cold. I should _____ _____ _____ _____. Otherwise I might get sick.

W Oh, the window of this room is open.

M Oh, really? I thought it was closed. I know _____ _____ _____ _____.

W Would you like me _____ _____ _____?

M _____

A Write down the definition of each word or phrase.

1	portable	11	groceries
2	feed	12	field trip
3	cage	13	improve
4	allowance	14	various
5	reservation	15	tend to
6	round trip	16	sneeze
7	charge	17	registered mail
8	upset	18	cherish
9	pleasure	19	lend
10	clerk	20	hardworking

B Match each word with the right definition.

1	stall	_____	a	외로운, 쓸쓸한
2	mean	_____	b	수술
3	miss	_____	c	(돈 등을) 쓰다, 소비하다, 들이다
4	operation	_____	d	소설
5	pay for	_____	e	~을 놓치다
6	customer	_____	f	편도의, 일방통행의
7	lonely	_____	g	실패
8	try on	_____	h	고객, 손님, 단골
9	put on	_____	i	~의 값을 지불하다
10	guidance	_____	j	매점
11	stomach	_____	k	~을 한번 입어보다
12	spend	_____	l	의미하다, 뜻하다
13	novel	_____	m	안내, 가르침
14	failure	_____	n	~을 입다, 걸치다
15	one way	_____	o	위, 배

C Choose the best answer for the blank.

1 It's very nice _____ you to make a copy of the book.

    a. for   b. to   c. of

2 I'm looking forward to _____ from you.

    a. hear   b. hearing   c. heard

3 We had better _____ to see a movie tonight.

    a. not go   b. not to go   c. don't go

4 _____ do you think of this novel?

    a. How   b. What   c. Why

5 I'm busy _____ on our science project.

    a. work   b. to work   c. working

6 He has _____ to Europe many times.

    a. gone   b. been   c. left

D Complete the short dialogues.

1 A: When do I have to submit the essay?

    B: You have to hand _____ your essay this Friday.

2 A: My name is John Smith.

    B: Let me _____. Yes, here is your reservation.

3 A: How was your vacation?

    B: I had _____ a pleasant time.

4 A: When do I have to leave?

    B: Leave right now, _____ you'll be late.

5 A: I forgot to lock the door yesterday.

    B: Right. Make _____ to lock the door when you leave home.

1 다음을 듣고, 남자가 지난 주말에 친구와 함께 구입한 것을 고르시오.

① clothes ② presents

③ notebooks ④ books

2 대화를 듣고, 남자의 직업으로 알맞은 것을 고르시오.

① copywriter ② stationery clerk

③ hotel receptionist ④ amateur photographer

3 다음을 듣고, 주어진 상황에서 할 수 있는 말로 가장 적절한 것을 고르시오.

① I can't hear you.

② Just do your best!

③ You did a great job.

④ You can do better next time.

4 대화를 듣고, 아빠가 딸에게 개를 산책시키라고 하는 이유를 고르시오.

① 개를 운동시켜야 해서

② 파티 준비를 해야 해서

③ 고모가 개를 무서워해서

④ 추수감사절 행사에 참여하기 위해서

5 대화를 듣고, 남자가 찾아가려고 하는 곳을 고르시오.

6 대화를 듣고, 남자가 추가로 가져올 것을 고르시오.

① potato ② cheese

③ cereal ④ flour

7 대화를 듣고, 여자가 전화를 한 목적을 고르시오.

① 연체된 비디오를 반납하라고

② 주문한 비디오를 가져가라고

③ 비디오 대여기간을 연장하려고

④ 최신 비디오가 있는지 물어보려고

8 대화를 듣고, 말하기 대회가 열리는 요일을 고르시오.

① Thursday

② Friday

③ Saturday

④ Sunday

9 대화를 듣고, 여자가 어젯밤에 한 일을 고르시오.

① 남자와 통화를 했다.

② 집에서 밤새 TV를 봤다.

③ 친구를 집에 초대했다.

④ 친구와 영화를 보러 갔다.

10 다음을 듣고, 두 사람의 대화가 <u>어색한</u> 것을 고르시오.

① ② ③ ④

11 대화를 듣고, 두 사람이 주문한 것들의 총액을 고르시오.

<Angelica's Dessert and Coffee House>

DRINKS		DESSERTS	
Coffee	$1.50	Cheesecake	$2.50(a slice)
Green Tea	$2.00	Cream cake	$2.50(a slice)
Milk	$1.50	Fruit	$4.00(a plate)
Juice (orange, grape, tomato)	$2.00	Pudding	$1.50

① $7.5 ② $8

③ $8.5 ④ $9

12 대화를 듣고, 남자가 지불해야 할 금액을 고르시오.

① $40
② $50
③ $70
④ $80

13 대화를 듣고, 남자의 심정으로 알맞은 것을 고르시오.

① 기대된다
② 초조하다
③ 무관심하다
④ 실망스럽다

14 대화를 듣고, 대화가 이루어지는 장소를 고르시오.

① 가구점
② 약국
③ 꽃가게
④ 과일가게

15 대화를 듣고, 무엇에 관한 내용인지 고르시오.

① 잘 자는 방법
② 다이어트 비법
③ 커피의 유해성
④ 일찍 일어나는 방법

16 다음을 듣고, 그림의 상황에 가장 알맞은 대화를 고르시오.

①   ②   ③   ④

17 대화를 듣고, 두 사람의 관계로 알맞은 것을 고르시오.

① 간호사 – 의사
② 점원 – 손님
③ 엄마 – 아들
④ 환자 – 약사

18 대화를 듣고, 내용과 일치하는 것을 고르시오.

① 여자는 괴물 이야기를 쓸 것이다.
② 남자는 가족 이야기를 쓸 것이다.
③ 여자의 이야기 속 남동생은 병으로 죽게 된다.
④ 남자가 쓰는 이야기의 주인공은 누나이다.

[19-20] 대화를 듣고, 남자의 마지막 말에 이어질 여자의 응답으로 가장 적절한 것을 고르시오.

19

① Baseball is more fun to me.
② I beat Yujin yesterday.
③ I didn't see you the day before.
④ I had to help my mom at home.

20

① OK. The day, the month, and then the year.
② So I write down June 10th 1995.
③ I was born at 2 o'clock in the morning.
④ Can you please spell it for me?

T E S T

9

1 다음을 듣고, 남자가 지난 주말에 친구와 함께 구입한 것을 고르시오.

① clothes
② presents
③ notebooks
④ books

M I went downtown with my friend last weekend. We went to a big bookstore and _____ _____ _____ . I bought two books and my friend bought three. Then we went and _____ _____ _____ . After eating, we went clothes shopping. But _____ _____ _____ any clothes. We didn't have much money.

2 대화를 듣고, 남자의 직업으로 알맞은 것을 고르시오.

① copywriter
② stationery clerk
③ hotel receptionist
④ amateur photographer

M Good afternoon. Can I help you?
W Yes, I'd like to _____ _____ _____ of these papers.
M Photocopies are 25 cents each.
W OK. Two copies, please.
M One moment. *[pause]* _____ _____ _____ anything else?
W Yes, I'd like to _____ _____ _____ .
M The total is $2.50.

3 다음을 듣고, 주어진 상황에서 할 수 있는 말로 가장 적절한 것을 고르시오.

① I can't hear you.
② Just do your best!
③ You did a great job.
④ You can do better next time.

M It's the day before the school's English speaking contest. Your friend is in the contest. _____ _____ _____ . You've listened to his speech. _____ _____ _____ . But your friend doesn't think _____ _____ _____ . You want to make him feel better. What would you say to him in this situation?

4 대화를 듣고, 아빠가 딸에게 개를 산책시키라고 하는 이유를 고르시오.

① 개를 운동시켜야 해서
② 파티 준비를 해야 해서
③ 고모가 개를 무서워해서
④ 추수감사절 행사에 참여하기 위해서

M Penny, take the dog to the park.
W But I took him _____ _____ _____ yesterday.
M Well, _____ _____ _____ in 10 minutes. We have something to talk to each other about this Thanksgiving party. But she hates dogs.
W Oh, that's right. She is _____ _____ _____ .
M So you take him for a walk for an hour.
W OK. Dad.

5 대화를 듣고, 남자가 찾아가려고 하는 곳을 고르시오.

[Cell phone rings.]

M Hello, it's me. Where are you?

W I'm at a PC room. Come and meet me.

M Where is it?

W _____ _____ _____ from our school and turn left. You'll see a hotel on your right. It's _____ _____ _____ past the hotel.

M Go two blocks and turn left. There will be a hotel on my right.

W That's right. The PC room is the second shop _____ _____ _____.

M OK. See you soon.

6 대화를 듣고, 남자가 추가로 가져올 것을 고르시오.

① potato
② cheese
③ cereal
④ flour

W Let's get in this line, Peter. I hope _____ _____ _____ we need.

M You made a shopping list, Mom. Why don't you check it?

W You're right. Now where is it? Oh, here it is... Let's see... Potatoes, tomatoes, cereal, flour... Oh, I didn't _____ _____ _____.

M I'll run and get some. You _____ _____ _____ _____.

W Thanks, Peter.

M No problem. Just a second.

7 대화를 듣고, 여자가 전화를 한 목적을 고르시오.

① 연체된 비디오를 반납하라고
② 주문한 비디오를 가져가라고
③ 비디오 대여기간을 연장하려고
④ 최신 비디오가 있는지 물어보려고

[Telephone rings.]

M Hello.

W Hello. Is this John Pauls?

M Yes, this is he speaking. Who's calling, please?

W Mr. Pauls, this is the Walnut Video Shop. You have two videos _____ _____ _____.

M Oh, I've completely forgot about that.

W They are two days overdue. Please _____ _____ _____.

M I will do it today. I'm sorry. By the way, do you have _____ _____ _____ starring Harrison Ford?

8 대화를 듣고, 말하기 대회가 열리는 요일을 고르시오.

① Thursday
② Friday
③ Saturday
④ Sunday

M The speech contest is _____ _____ _____ .

W Then it is on Saturday.

M No, it's not on Saturday.

W But today is Tuesday and four days from now is Saturday.

M Today isn't Tuesday. _____ _____ _____ . You told me you went on a picnic with your family yesterday.

W Oh, sorry, _____ _____ _____ .

M Do you know when the speech contest is, now?

9 대화를 듣고, 여자가 어젯밤에 한 일을 고르시오.

① 남자와 통화를 했다.
② 집에서 밤새 TV를 봤다.
③ 친구를 집에 초대했다.
④ 친구와 영화를 보러 갔다.

M I thought you were going to stay home last night. I called you, but _____ _____ _____ .

W I was going to watch TV all night. But Jane called.

M _____ _____ _____ _____ ?

W Yes, she invited me to a movie. But it was a bad movie. _____ _____ _____ _____ .

10 다음을 듣고, 두 사람의 대화가 어색한 것을 고르시오.

①   ②   ③   ④

① **W** I'm sorry, I took _____ _____ _____ .
   M That's why you are so late.
② **W** These chocolates look delicious.
   M _____ _____ , please.
③ **W** What does _____ _____ _____ ?
   M She is tall with long hair.
④ **W** It was really nice to see you again.
   M OK. I'll _____ _____ _____ .

11 대화를 듣고, 두 사람이 주문한 것들의 총액을 고르시오.

〈Angelica's Desert and Coffee House 〉

DRINKS		DESSERTS	
Coffee	$1.50	Cheesecake	$2.50(a slice)
Green Tea	$2.00	Cream cake	$2.50(a slice)
Milk	$1.50	Fruit	$4.00(a plate)
Juice (orange, grape, tomato)	$2.00	Pudding	$1.50

① $7.5   ② $8
③ $8.5   ④ $9

M The coffee _____ _____ _____ . I'd like a cup of coffee. How about you?

W I don't drink coffee. I'd like _____ _____ _____ .

M OK. I'll order a coffee and a juice. Would you like a dessert?

W Of course. I love to have some cheesecake.

M And I'll have _____ _____ _____ . Just sit here. I'll go and get the drinks and dessert.

12 대화를 듣고, 남자가 지불해야 할 금액을 고르시오.

① $40
② $50
③ $70
④ $80

W Hello. How may I help you?

M Well, I'm _____ _____ _____ _____ for my teacher.

W We have many kinds of ties.

M I like this necktie. How much is it?

W The regular price is $40, but _____ _____ _____ for $25.

M Really? _____ _____ _____ _____ . I think my father likes them, too.

W Good. You made a great choice.

13 대화를 듣고, 남자의 심정으로 알맞은 것을 고르시오.

① 기대된다
② 초조하다
③ 무관심하다
④ 실망스럽다

M Where are we going _____ _____ , Mom?

W Camping. We'll go camping for one week.

M I thought you said we would go to Disneyland. Daddy promised me _____ _____ _____ !

W We can't this year. _____ _____ _____ . And camping will be great.

M That's too bad. I really want to go to Disneyland.

14 대화를 듣고, 대화가 이루어지는 장소를 고르시오.

① 가구점
② 약국
③ 꽃가게
④ 과일가게

M How much are they?

W They are $3 _____ _____ .

M Are they sweet? I bought some apples last week, they weren't good.

W Yes, the tomatoes are _____ _____ _____ _____ . Look how red they are.

M OK. I'll have that basket there. And I need some oranges, too.

W I have _____ _____ _____ over here.

M I'll have 20. By the way, would you tell me _____ _____ _____ _____ is around here?

15 대화를 듣고, 무엇에 관한 내용인지 고르시오.

① 잘 자는 방법
② 다이어트 비법
③ 커피의 유해성
④ 일찍 일어나는 방법

W I'm so sleepy now. I can't sleep well _____ _____
_____.

M Why do you think you can't sleep?

W I don't know.

M Do you _____ _____? Or do you drink coffee at night?

W No, I don't. Should I go see a doctor?

M Before going to see a doctor, _____ _____ _____
before you go to bed. _____ _____ _____ _____.
And drink a glass of warm milk. You will sleep better.

16 다음을 듣고, 그림의 상황에 가장 알맞은 대화를 고르시오.

① ② ③ ④

① **M** Have you ever been to Thailand?

W No. Are you _____ _____ _____ _____ for a
vacation?

② **M** Hey, you're Anne, right?

W Yes, but I'm sorry, do you know me?

③ **M** _____ _____ _____ to Customer Service.

W Do you want to _____ _____ _____?

④ **M** How much is this CD?

W Ten thousand won, but it's 20% off right now.

17 대화를 듣고, 두 사람의 관계로 알맞은 것을 고르시오.

① 간호사 – 의사
② 점원 – 손님
③ 엄마 – 아들
④ 환자 – 약사

M Here is _____ _____.

W Thank you. You went to see a doctor because of a stomachache.
[pause] _____ _____ _____ medicine here before?

M Yes, I have.

W Yes, I see your name on the computer now. It will take me 10
minutes to _____ _____ _____.

M I will wait here.

18 대화를 듣고, 내용과 일치하는 것을 고르시오.

① 여자는 괴물 이야기를 쓸 것이다.
② 남자는 가족 이야기를 쓸 것이다.
③ 여자의 이야기 속 남동생은 병으로 죽게 된다.
④ 남자가 쓰는 이야기의 주인공은 누나이다.

M We have to hand in the writing assignment next Monday, which I _____ _____ _____ !
W I'll start it today.
M Do you have any good ideas for your story?
W Yes, I will write a story about a sister _____ _____ _____ .
M How does he die?
W He has _____ _____ _____ . What about you?
M I think I will write a story about a monster.
W _____ _____ _____ .

19 대화를 듣고, 남자의 마지막 말에 이어질 여자의 응답으로 가장 적절한 것을 고르시오.

① Baseball is more fun to me.
② I beat Yujin yesterday.
③ I didn't see you the day before.
④ I had to help my mom at home.

M What's your _____ _____ ?
W Basketball.
M Really? I didn't think _____ _____ _____ .
W I often play with Yujin after school.
M Yujin is very good at it. _____ _____ _____ _____ yesterday after school.
W Yes, she is very good.
M Where were you yesterday?
W _____

20 대화를 듣고, 남자의 마지막 말에 이어질 여자의 응답으로 가장 적절한 것을 고르시오.

① OK. The day, the month, and then the year.
② So I write down June 10th 1995.
③ I was born at 2 o'clock in the morning.
④ Can you please spell it for me?

M Will you _____ _____ _____ _____ , please?
W Yes. Let's see... It says 'Date of Birth.'
M Yes, put your _____ _____ _____ there.
W Do I write down the day, the month, and then the year?
M No, _____ _____ _____ _____ , the day, and then the year.
W _____

1 다음을 듣고, 그림의 상황에 가장 알맞은 대화를 고르시오.

① ② ③ ④

2 다음을 듣고, 무엇에 관한 내용인지 고르시오.
① meat
② healthy food
③ healthful exercise
④ vegetables and fruits

3 대화를 듣고, 여자가 남자를 위해 해줄 일을 고르시오.
① 약 사다 주기
② 재킷 갖다 주기
③ 병원에 같이 가기
④ 약을 처방해 주기

4 대화를 듣고, 내용과 일치하지 않는 것을 고르시오.
① 남자는 야구를 한 후, 방 청소를 하고 싶어한다.
② 엄마는 야구보다 방 청소를 먼저 하길 바란다.
③ 남자는 야구를 한 후, 방을 청소할 것이다.
④ 남자는 방 청소를 하고 나서, 야구를 할 것이다.

5 대화를 듣고, 두 사람이 보기로 한 방송 프로그램을 고르시오.
① comedy
② interview show
③ police drama
④ documentary

6 대화를 듣고, 두 사람이 현재 있는 장소를 고르시오.
① 도서 대여점
② 학교
③ 도서관
④ 서점

7 다음을 듣고, 두 사람의 대화가 어색한 것을 고르시오.
① ② ③ ④

8 다음을 듣고, 내용에 가장 알맞은 안내문을 고르시오.
① RECYCLE PLASTICS
② DON'T BE A LITTERBUG
③ REDUCE FOOD GARBAGE
④ REDUCE, REUSE, AND RECYCLE

9 대화를 듣고, 여자의 장래희망으로 알맞은 것을 고르시오.
① fire fighter
② police officer
③ car racer
④ soldier

10 대화를 듣고, 남자에 관한 내용으로 알맞지 않은 것을 고르시오.
① 체중감량을 하고 있다.
② 밤에는 피곤해서 운동을 안 한다.
③ 건강에 좋은 음식을 먹지 않는다.
④ 아침에 일어나서 운동을 한다.

11 다음을 듣고, 무엇에 관한 설명인지 고르시오.

① 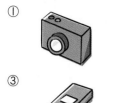   ②

③   ④

12 대화를 듣고, 여자가 남자에게 전화를 건 목적을 고르시오.

① 약을 좀 사오라고
② 병원에 데려 가려고
③ 데리러 가지 못한다고
④ 병원에 예약을 하려고

13 대화를 듣고, 두 사람의 관계로 알맞은 것을 고르시오.

① husband ····· wife
② teacher ····· mother
③ mother ····· son
④ teacher ····· student

14 대화를 듣고, 남자의 마지막 말의 의도로 알맞은 것을 고르시오.

① 조언 요청
② 충고
③ 의심
④ 비난

15 대화를 듣고, 남자와 여자가 만나기로 한 시각으로 알맞은 것을 고르시오.

① 6:00
② 6:30
③ 7:00
④ 7:30

16 대화를 듣고, 여자와 남자의 심경으로 가장 알맞은 것을 고르시오.

① excited
② bored
③ well-rested
④ tired

17 대화를 듣고, 남자가 걱정하는 것을 고르시오.

① 가격이 싸면 질이 좋지 않을까봐
② 겨울에는 가격이 비쌀까봐
③ 올 겨울 유행에 맞지 않을까봐
④ 옷에 돈을 너무 많이 쓸까봐

18 다음을 듣고, 요일별 날씨가 바르게 연결되지 <u>않은</u> 것을 고르시오.

① 금요일 − 비가 오는
② 토요일 − 화창한
③ 일요일 − 화창한
④ 월요일 − 뜨거운

[19~20] 대화를 듣고, 남자의 마지막 말에 이어질 여자의 응답으로 가장 적절한 것을 고르시오.

19

① Thank you. That's kind of you.
② Sorry. Could you repeat yourself?
③ My house is bigger than yours.
④ It's OK. This seat is empty.

20

① To the library.
② To buy some books.
③ I'm going home.
④ Hurry up! You're late!

1 다음을 듣고, 그림의 상황에 가장 알맞은 대화를 고르시오.

① **W** May I take your order?

M Would you _____ _____ _____?

② **W** Can you _____ _____, please?

M Yes, I will put everything in the toy box.

③ **W** Thanks for helping me _____ _____ _____, Billy.

M No problem, Sarah. I'll always help you.

④ **W** Where are you going?

M To the library. I need to help my friend with homework.

① ② ③ ④

2 다음을 듣고, 무엇에 관한 내용인지 고르시오.

① meat
② healthy food
③ healthful exercise
④ vegetables and fruits

W Fresh vegetables and fruits are the healthiest foods. Cooking them destroys vitamins. Cooked vegetables are not as healthy as uncooked ones. To be healthy, you should also eat lots of grains _____ _____ _____ _____. But you don't need to eat a lot of meat. Just _____ _____ _____ _____ is enough.

3 대화를 듣고, 여자가 남자를 위해 해줄 일을 고르시오.

① 약 사다 주기
② 재킷 갖다 주기
③ 병원에 같이 가기
④ 약을 처방해 주기

M I feel sick. My stomach is upset.

W Oh, really? Since when? What did you have?

M Since this morning. I didn't have _____ _____. Can you get me something _____ _____ _____?

W Let's just go to _____ _____ _____.

M OK. Let me get my jacket.

4 대화를 듣고, 내용과 일치하지 <u>않는</u> 것을 고르시오.

① 남자는 야구를 한 후, 방 청소를 하고 싶어한다.
② 엄마는 야구보다 방 청소를 먼저 하길 바란다.
③ 남자는 야구를 한 후, 방을 청소할 것이다.
④ 남자는 방 청소를 하고 나서, 야구를 할 것이다.

M Mom, can I go out and play baseball?

W You must clean your room first.

M But the game is _____ _____ _____ _____. Can I clean my room after I play?

W _____, _____ _____. I want you to clean your room before you play.

M OK. _____ _____ _____ right now.

5 대화를 듣고, 두 사람이 보기로 한 방송 프로그램을 고르시오.

① comedy
② interview show
③ police drama
④ documentary

M Are you watching a police drama on TV?

W Yes, I love to watch police dramas.

M _____ _____ _____. Can we watch something else?

W I don't like _____ _____ _____ which you like.

M OK. Then let's watch a comedy. Are there _____ _____ _____?

W Yes, *Six Men in the House*. I like it, so I'll _____ _____ _____.

M Thanks.

6 대화를 듣고, 두 사람이 현재 있는 장소를 고르시오.

① 도서 대여점
② 학교
③ 도서관
④ 서점

M Oh, _____ _____ _____ I need.

W How much is it?

M It's $12.

W Do you _____ _____ _____?

M Yes, I do. I _____ _____ _____ in the library, but I didn't see it.

W So you have to buy it.

M That's right.

7 다음을 듣고, 두 사람의 대화가 <u>어색한</u> 것을 고르시오.

①   ②   ③   ④

① M What is your favorite food?
   W _____ _____ _____ like Italian food.

② M I lost my book _____ _____ _____ _____ _____.
   W I'll help you look for it.

③ M What do you want to be in the future?
   W I want to be a doctor.

④ M What do you like to do _____ _____?
   W I like to ride my bicycle with my sister.

8 다음을 듣고, 내용에 가장 알맞은 안내문을 고르시오.

① RECYCLE PLASTICS
② DON'T BE A LITTERBUG
③ REDUCE FOOD GARBAGE
④ REDUCE, REUSE, AND RECYCLE

M There is too much garbage in our world. You should recycle paper, plastic, cans and bottles. Put cans and bottles _____ _____ _____ _____. And you should do other things. Every house has _____ _____ _____ _____. When you buy something, _____ _____ _____ you don't need a plastic bag.

9 대화를 듣고, 여자의 장래희망으로 알맞은 것을 고르시오.

① fire fighter
② police officer
③ car racer
④ soldier

M I am happy, but I am worried.
W Dad, I want to do what you do. You help people every day.
M Yes, _____ _____ _____ to people. And I stop drivers who are driving too fast.
W And _____ _____ _____?
M Yes, I catch robbers and thieves. It can be dangerous.
W Don't worry, Dad. More and more women are _____ _____ _____.

10 대화를 듣고, 남자에 관한 내용으로 알맞지 <u>않은</u> 것을 고르시오.

① 체중감량을 하고 있다.
② 밤에는 피곤해서 운동을 안 한다.
③ 건강에 좋은 음식을 먹지 않는다.
④ 아침에 일어나서 운동을 한다.

M _____ _____ _____ _____ _____ _____.
W Do you exercise?
M I'm too tired at night. I want to watch TV.
W Are you _____ _____ _____?
M Not really. Healthy food is not delicious.
W If you really want to lose weight, you would do it _____ _____ _____ _____.

11 다음을 듣고, 무엇에 관한 설명인지 고르시오.

① ② ③ ④

M This is _____ _____ _____. It can be carried from place to place easily. It is thin and a few centimeters long. It is _____ _____ _____ _____. Information or pictures are moved from the computer to this device. It stores or _____ _____ _____. Then, the information can be easily moved to another computer.

12 대화를 듣고, 여자가 남자에게 전화를 건 목적을 고르시오.

① 약을 좀 사오라고
② 병원에 데려 가려고
③ 데리러 가지 못한다고
④ 병원에 예약을 하려고

[Cell phone rings.]

M Hello.

W Mike, this is Mom. You'll have to _____ _____ _____ _____ from soccer practice today.

M _____ _____ _____ _____ _____ ?

W No, I have a doctor's appointment.

M You have a doctor's appointment? Is something wrong?

W My back is _____ _____ _____ . Too much housework. So I want to get some medicine.

13 대화를 듣고, 두 사람의 관계로 알맞은 것을 고르시오.

① husband ..... wife
② teacher ..... mother
③ mother ..... son
④ teacher ..... student

M He always does his homework, and _____ _____ .

W That's good to hear.

M But your son talks too much in class.

W I know. He likes to _____ _____ _____ .

M Well, _____ _____ _____ _____ yesterday, because he was talking too much in class.

W He talks a lot _____ _____ , too. What should I do about him?

14 대화를 듣고, 남자의 마지막 말의 의도로 알맞은 것을 고르시오.

① 조언 요청
② 충고
③ 의심
④ 비난

M I have already spent all my allowance this week. I always don't have _____ _____ _____ .

W Do you want to save some money?

M Yes, I do. How much of your allowance do you save?

W I save _____ _____ _____ .

M Half? Are you _____ _____ _____ ? How is that possible?

15 대화를 듣고, 남자와 여자가 만나기로 한 시각으로 알맞은 것을 고르시오.

① 6:00
② 6:30
③ 7:00
④ 7:30

M What time _____ _____ _____ _____ today?
W Can you meet me at 6:00?
M _____ _____ _____ _____ until 7:30.
W I want to have dinner first.
M But I can't meet you at 6:00. _____ _____ _____ _____ until 6:30.
W OK. Let's meet at 7:00. We will eat after the show.

16 대화를 듣고, 여자와 남자의 심경으로 가장 알맞은 것을 고르시오.

① excited
② bored
③ well-rested
④ tired

M Long car trips are _____ _____.
W Yes, there is nothing to do.
M I can't read because it _____ _____ _____ _____.
W We can only sit and _____ _____ _____ _____.
M Nine hours of looking out the window is not fun.

17 대화를 듣고, 남자가 걱정하는 것을 고르시오.

① 가격이 싸면 질이 좋지 않을까봐
② 겨울에는 가격이 비쌀까봐
③ 올 겨울 유행에 맞지 않을까봐
④ 옷에 돈을 너무 많이 쓸까봐

M Kathy, where are you going?
W Come here. Look at the sign. 80% off.
M _____ _____. It's the middle of August.
W I know, but the price is perfect. 80% off.
M But the style will not _____ _____ _____ this coming winter.
W I should _____ _____ _____. The price is so low.

18 다음을 듣고, 요일별 날씨가 바르게 연결되지 <u>않은</u> 것을 고르시오.

① 금요일 – 비가 오는
② 토요일 – 화창한
③ 일요일 – 화창한
④ 월요일 – 뜨거운

W Good evening. Here's the weather forecast. Today it was rainy. _____ _____ _____ _____ _____. Tomorrow is Saturday and everyone wants to go outside, but the weather will be the same tomorrow _____ _____ _____ _____.
But Sunday will be very hot and sunny. So you can go to the beach. The heat will _____ _____ _____ _____ half of next week.

19 대화를 듣고, 남자의 마지막 말에 이어질 여자의 응답으로 가장 적절한 것을 고르시오.

① Thank you. That's kind of you.
② Sorry. Could you repeat yourself?
③ My house is bigger than yours.
④ It's OK. This seat is empty.

W Thanks for _____ _____ _____ to watch the game.
M Well, we both love soccer. It will be fun to _____ _____ _____.
W I brought some snacks.
M Great. I'll get some drinks. Just go in the living room.
W OK.
M And _____ _____ _____ _____.
W _____

20 대화를 듣고, 남자의 마지막 말에 이어질 여자의 응답으로 가장 적절한 것을 고르시오.

① To the library.
② To buy some books.
③ I'm going home.
④ Hurry up! You're late!

M You look like you're in a hurry.
W Yes, _____ _____ _____ _____ now.
M Where are you going?
W I have to _____ _____ _____ right now.
M Excuse me? Did you say you're going to the bookstore?
W _____, _____ _____.
M Where are you going, then?
W _____

WORD AND EXPRESSION REVIEW • TEST 9-10

A Write down the definition of each word or phrase.

1 nervous

2 scared (of)

3 line-up

4 latest

5 amazing

6 in fashion

7 ripe

8 prescription

9 spell

10 wheat

11 pharmacy

12 personally

13 garbage

14 reduce

15 criminal

16 decide to

17 device

18 sore

19 by the way

20 thief

B Match each word with the right definition.

1 plate   _____

2 healthful   _____

3 beat   _____

4 scary   _____

5 recycle   _____

6 register   _____

7 store   _____

8 say   _____

9 assignment   _____

10 force   _____

11 complaint   _____

12 fill out   _____

13 overdue   _____

14 flour   _____

15 litterbug   _____

a 밀가루

b 지불기한이 넘은, 늦은

c 접시

d 등록하다

e 불만, 불평

f 과제, 숙제

g 무서운

h 패배시키다, 이기다

i 기입하다, 써넣다

j ~라고 쓰여 있다

k 건강에 좋은, 유익한

l 재활용하다, 재생하여 이용하다

m (공공장소에서) 쓰레기 버리는 사람

n (세력) 단체, ~대, 경찰(대)

o 저장하다

C Choose the best answer for the blank.

1 You promised me _____ me there!

a. take   b. to take   c. taking

2 It will _____ you 1 hour to get there.

a. spend   b. give   c. take

3 His shoes are the same size _____ mine.

a. as   b. to   c. with

4 You have to _____ a doctor right now.

a. meet   b. look at   c. see

5 It _____ fun.

a. sounds   b. sounds like   c. sounds of

6 There is a hotel _____ my right.

a. on   b. of   c. from

D Complete the short dialogues.

1 A: What does she _____ _____?

B: She is tall with long hair.

2 A: Hi, Jenny. Thank you for inviting me.

B: Welcome to my home. Make yourself _____ _____.

3 A: I think you're late for school.

B: That's why I'm _____ a hurry now.

4 A: He's got a better grade in English.

B: That's good to _____.

5 A: I lost my book on my _____ to school.

B: I'll help you look for it.

1 다음을 듣고, 상황에 맞는 그림을 고르시오.

①

②

③

④

2 대화를 듣고, 영화에 대해 알 수 <u>없는</u> 것을 고르시오.

① 연기
② 음향효과
③ 특수효과
④ 줄거리

3 대화를 듣고, 인터넷 쇼핑이 <u>어려운</u> 물건을 고르시오.

① 신발
② 가방
③ 옷
④ 음식

4 대화를 듣고, 남자가 지금부터 하게 될 일을 고르시오.

① to go home
② to go shopping
③ to make some food
④ to do his homework

5 대화를 듣고, 두 사람의 관계가 바르게 짝지어진 것을 고르시오.

① 교사 – 학생
② 학부모 – 교사
③ 교사 – 교사
④ 엄마 – 아빠

6 대화를 듣고, 무엇에 관한 내용인지 고르시오.

① 남자의 통근 시간
② 남자의 귀가 시간
③ 남자의 기상 시간
④ 남자의 아침 식사 시간

7 다음을 듣고, 남자가 서점에서 구입한 것을 고르시오.

①

②

③

④

8 대화를 듣고, 남자가 라면을 끓일 때 사용하지 <u>않는</u> 재료를 고르시오.

① 떡
② 파
③ 김치
④ 계란

9 대화를 듣고, 남자가 여자에게 돈을 빌리는 목적을 고르시오.

① 책을 사려고
② 공책을 사려고
③ 친구 돈을 갚으려고
④ 시험 응시료를 내려고

10 대화를 듣고, 여자가 차를 운전한 속도를 고르시오.

① 20km
② 50km
③ 70km
④ 80km

11 대화를 듣고, 여자가 찾아가고자 하는 곳을 지도에서 고르시오.

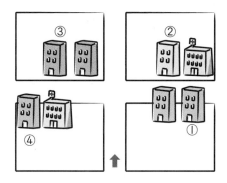

12 다음을 듣고, 두 사람의 대화가 <u>어색한</u> 것을 고르시오.

①   ②   ③   ④

13 대화를 듣고, 셔츠 값으로 남자가 지불해야 할 금액을 고르시오.

① $20
② $22
③ $23
④ $25

14 다음을 듣고, 남자가 가장 싫어하는 과목을 고르시오.

① 미술
② 음악
③ 수학
④ 체육

15 대화를 듣고, 두 사람이 지금 하려고 하는 일을 고르시오.

① 중국 음식점에 가기
② 한국 음식 먹으러 가기
③ 통닭 시켜먹기
④ 초밥 먹으러 가기

16 다음을 듣고, 주어진 상황에서 할 수 있는 말로 가장 적절한 것을 고르시오.

① Thanks for inviting me.
② Please come again.
③ See you. Thanks for coming.
④ Please come in.

17 다음을 듣고, 그림의 상황에 가장 알맞은 대화를 고르시오.

①   ②   ③   ④

18 대화를 듣고, 남자의 심경으로 가장 알맞은 것을 고르시오.

① bored
② upset
③ surprised
④ pleased

[19-20] 대화를 듣고, 여자의 마지막 말에 이어질 남자의 응답으로 가장 적절한 것을 고르시오.

19

① That's good to hear.
② Are you hot right now?
③ Oh, that's too bad.
④ Is it very hot today?

20

① I can carry them with easy.
② Walk inside quickly.
③ You are a good friend.
④ They are too heavy to move.

DICTATION ● TEST 11

1 다음을 듣고, 상황에 맞는 그림을 고르시오.

① ② ③ ④

W James is walking home after his guitar lesson. _____ _____ _____ _____ the guitar teacher's house. On the way home James _____ _____ _____, Jessica. He says hello to Jessica. Jessica is _____ _____ _____, so James _____ _____ and says hello, too.

2 대화를 듣고, 영화에 대해 알 수 <u>없는</u> 것을 고르시오.

① 연기
② 음향효과
③ 특수효과
④ 줄거리

M That movie was terrible.
W _____ _____ _____ _____?
M No, the acting was OK. And the story was OK, too.
W What was the problem then?
M It was the special effects. It was like _____ _____ _____.
W Yes, _____ _____ _____ were terrible.

3 대화를 듣고, 인터넷 쇼핑이 <u>어려운</u> 물건을 고르시오.

① 신발
② 가방
③ 옷
④ 음식

M Shopping on the Internet is easy.
W Yes, it is. _____ _____ _____ _____ going to a store.
M Yes, I think so.
W But there are some things that _____ _____ _____ _____ on the Internet.
M Yes, _____. You might buy the wrong size.
W I couldn't _____ _____ _____ _____.

4 대화를 듣고, 남자가 지금부터 하게 될 일을 고르시오.

① to go home
② to go shopping
③ to make some food
④ to do his homework

W Hi, I'm home.
M Hi, Mom.
W What did you do after school today? Did you _____ _____ _____?
M No, I went shopping. I needed some _____ _____ _____ _____ for school.
W OK.
M I'm going to do it now.
W OK. I'll _____ _____ _____ for you.

5 대화를 듣고, 두 사람의 관계가 바르게 짝지어진 것을 고르시오.

① 교사 – 학생
② 학부모 – 교사
③ 교사 – 교사
④ 엄마 – 아빠

M Do you know Lisa? She is a very good student.
W She always tries very hard.
M She does very well on the test _____ _____ _____.
W And she does well on the test in my class, too.
M _____ _____ _____ and kind to classmates. Her mother and father should _____ _____ _____ _____.

6 대화를 듣고, 무엇에 관한 내용인지 고르시오.

① 남자의 통근 시간
② 남자의 귀가 시간
③ 남자의 기상 시간
④ 남자의 아침 식사 시간

M Thanks for this breakfast. Oh, I'll be home after 9 p.m. today.
W After nine? Are you _____ _____ _____?
M Yes, I am. I have something to finish this week.
W Please hurry home. You _____ _____ _____ _____ all week.
M Honey, we're really busy at work.

7 다음을 듣고, 남자가 서점에서 구입한 것을 고르시오.

① ② ③ ④

M Andy went shopping in the bookstore _____ _____ _____ _____ from school. He needed to buy a science book. But the bookstore didn't have the book he needed. _____ _____ _____ _____ _____. But he bought _____ _____ _____ _____. He has to go to another bookstore.

8 대화를 듣고, 남자가 라면을 끓일 때 사용하지 <u>않는</u> 재료를 고르시오.

① 떡
② 파
③ 김치
④ 계란

W What can you cook?

M Not much. I can make noodles.

W _____ _____! Everyone can do that.

M Well, I can make it very delicious. I always _____ _____ _____ and some green onions in it, too.

W Anything else? Do you put kimchi in it?

M No. I sometimes put some _____ _____ _____ _____ in it.

9 대화를 듣고, 남자가 여자에게 돈을 빌리는 목적을 고르시오.

① 책을 사려고
② 공책을 사려고
③ 친구 돈을 갚으려고
④ 시험 응시료를 내려고

M Hello, Karen. Do you have any money on you?

W Just a little. Why do you ask?

M _____ _____ _____ 10,000 won? I need to buy a book after school. I have to _____ _____ _____ tonight. It will help me for the test tomorrow. I will give you back the money tomorrow.

W OK. I will _____ _____ _____ _____ if you are buying a book.

M Thank you.

10 대화를 듣고, 여자가 차를 운전한 속도를 고르시오.

① 20km
② 50km
③ 70km
④ 80km

M Excuse me, ma'am, _____ _____ _____ 20km over the speed limit.

W _____ _____ _____ _____ 60km an hour?

M No, it's only 50km an hour.

W Oh, really? _____ _____ _____ _____. Will you have to give me a ticket?

M Yes, I will, ma'am.

11 대화를 듣고, 여자가 찾아가고자 하는 곳을 지도에서 고르시오.

W Excuse me. Where is _____ _____ _____?

M A bank? Hmm... OK. Go straight one block and turn left. It's _____ _____ _____ on your right. It's across from a hospital.

W Let me check. I go one block and turn left. The bank is the second building _____ _____ _____.

M That's right.

W Thank you.

12 다음을 듣고, 두 사람의 대화가 <u>어색한 것</u>을 고르시오.

① ② ③ ④

① **W** Could you _____ _____ _____ _____ ?

   M I don't know the time.

② **W** It's going to rain today.

   M I will _____ _____ _____ .

③ **W** May I help you?

   M Yes, please. I want these shoes in a larger size.

④ **W** _____ _____ _____ my birthday?

   M No, I didn't. Happy Birthday! Here is your present.

13 대화를 듣고, 셔츠 값으로 남자가 지불해야 할 금액을 고르시오.

① $20
② $22
③ $23
④ $25

W There are two kinds of _____ _____ . One is the state government and the other is _____ _____ _____ .

M How much are they?

W The state sales tax is 6 percent and the national sales tax is 4 percent. You should _____ _____ _____ .

M So how much will I have to pay for this $20 shirt?

14 다음을 듣고, 남자가 가장 싫어하는 과목을 고르시오.

① 미술
② 음악
③ 수학
④ 체육

M My mother is an artist. She taught me how to _____ _____ _____ . So I really love art class at school. I also like music class. I, however, do not like _____ _____ . I am not very strong. And I can't run fast. So physical education is the class _____ _____ _____ _____ .

15 대화를 듣고, 두 사람이 지금 하려고 하는 일을 고르시오.

① 중국 음식점에 가기
② 한국 음식 먹으러 가기
③ 통닭 시켜먹기
④ 초밥 먹으러 가기

M Let's go have lunch. I want fried chicken.
W _____ _____ _____ for me.
M Chinese food then?
W No, I want to _____ _____ _____. You should pick a different restaurant.
M OK. Let's go _____ _____ _____.
W That's a good idea. It's healthy food.

16 다음을 듣고, 주어진 상황에서 할 수 있는 말로 가장 적절한 것을 고르시오.

① Thanks for inviting me.
② Please come again.
③ See you. Thanks for coming.
④ Please come in.

W _____ _____ _____ on Bill's front door. Bill thinks it is John. Yesterday Bill invited John to come to his house _____ _____ _____. Bill answers the door. It is John. They both say hello. Then Bill wants to tell John to _____ _____ _____. What would Bill say to John?

17 다음을 듣고, 그림의 상황에 가장 알맞은 대화를 고르시오.

①　　②　　③　　④

① M Excuse me, ma'am. You forgot to write down your address.
　　W Oh, I'm sorry. I'll write it right now.
② M I heard that _____ _____ _____ to the University. Congratulations!
　　W Thanks! _____ _____ _____.
③ M Good evening. What seems to be the problem?
　　W Well, I'm feeling pain _____ _____ _____.
④ M What are you doing _____ _____?
　　W I'm giving you medical treatment soon.

18 대화를 듣고, 남자의 심경으로 가장 알맞은 것을 고르시오.

① bored
② upset
③ surprised
④ pleased

M My team lost the soccer game.
W Oh, that's too bad.
M _____ _____ _____ _____ 0-0. And my team was playing really well.
W Then why did your team lose?
M The referee gave the other team _____ _____ _____. But it wasn't an _____ _____ at all.
W So, you're saying that the referee _____ _____ _____.
M Yes! I really think so.

19 대화를 듣고, 여자의 마지막 말에 이어질 남자의 응답으로 가장 적절한 것을 고르시오.

① That's good to hear.
② Are you hot right now?
③ Oh, that's too bad.
④ Is it very hot today?

M Hi, I'm looking for Peter. Do you know where he is?
W He _____ _____ _____ school today.
M What is wrong with him? _____ _____ _____?
W Yes, he is. I called him last night. And he said he had _____ _____ _____.
M _____

20 대화를 듣고, 여자의 마지막 말에 이어질 남자의 응답으로 가장 적절한 것을 고르시오.

① I can carry them with ease.
② Walk inside quickly.
③ You are a good friend.
④ They are too heavy to move.

W Could you please help me now?
M Yes, of course. Do you need me to _____ _____ _____ _____ for you?
W Yes. [pause] Thank you. Now can you _____ _____ _____?
M Yes, I can.
W These boxes are _____ _____.
M Don't worry. _____

1 다음을 듣고, 그림을 가장 적절하게 묘사한 것을 고르시오.

① ② ③ ④

2 다음을 듣고, 남자가 어렸을 때 했던 일을 순서대로 나열한 것을 고르시오.

(A) (B)

(C)

① (A)-(B)-(C)   ② (A)-(C)-(B)
③ (B)-(A)-(C)   ④ (C)-(B)-(A)

3 대화를 듣고, 어떤 상황에서 이루어지는 대화인지 고르시오.

① 음식 주문하기
② 음식 맛 평가하기
③ 맛있는 식당 추천하기
④ 수프 조리법 소개하기

4 대화를 듣고, 남자가 주말에 한 일이 <u>아닌</u> 것을 고르시오.

① 채소 따기   ② 음식 만들기
③ 시골에 가기   ④ 채소밭일 돕기

5 다음을 듣고, 무엇에 관한 안내인지 고르시오

① 영어 회화 시험
② 교사와의 학업 상담
③ 담임 선생님 연락처
④ 영어 작문 대회

6 대화를 듣고, 여자의 장래희망으로 알맞은 것을 고르시오.

① scientist   ② accountant
③ banker   ④ math teacher

7 다음을 듣고, 두 사람의 대화가 <u>어색한</u> 것을 고르시오.

① ② ③ ④

8 대화를 듣고, 여자가 남자에게 전화를 건 목적을 고르시오.

① 버스 정류장의 위치를 물어보려고
② 버스의 출발 시간을 물어보려고
③ 버스 번호가 몇 번인지 물어보려고
④ 도착지까지의 소요시간을 물어보려고

9 다음을 듣고, 남자에게 어울리는 속담으로 알맞은 것을 고르시오.

① All roads lead to Rome.
② When in Rome do as the Romans do.
③ A little knowledge is a dangerous thing.
④ Rome was not built in a day.

10 다음을 듣고, 여자가 여름에 하는 일이 <u>아닌</u> 것을 고르시오.

① 일광욕하기   ② 수영하기
③ 아르바이트 하기   ④ 바비큐 해먹기

11 다음을 듣고, 무엇에 관한 설명인지 고르시오.

① ②

③ ④

12 다음을 듣고, 이어폰으로 음악을 들을 때 주의해야 할 점으로 언급된 것을 고르시오.

① 소리를 작게 해서 듣기
② 다른 사람들에게 방해가 되지 않게 듣기
③ 한쪽으로 듣지 말고 양쪽으로 듣기
④ 좋은 이어폰으로 듣기

13 다음을 듣고, 주어진 상황에서 할 수 있는 말로 가장 적절한 것을 고르시오.

① Your father is proud of you.
② My father is very healthy.
③ Let me know if I can help.
④ Long time no see.

14 다음을 듣고, 게시물의 내용과 일치하지 <u>않는</u> 것을 고르시오.

Rules for riding the roller coaster:

• Take off your backpack and hat before sitting down.
• Leave your hat and backpack at the entrance.
• Do not throw things to the ground while the coaster is going.
• Children under 120 cm tall are not allowed to ride it.

---

①   ②   ③   ④

15 대화를 듣고, Brian의 생일이 며칠 남았는지 고르시오.

① 7일   ② 13일
③ 17일   ④ 30일

16 대화를 듣고, 남자가 하는 말의 의도로 알맞은 것을 고르시오

① 칭찬   ② 권유
③ 질투   ④ 명령

17 다음을 듣고, 도표의 내용과 일치하지 <u>않는</u> 것을 고르시오.

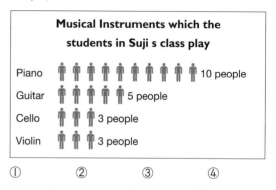

Musical Instruments which the students in Suji s class play	
Piano	10 people
Guitar	5 people
Cello	3 people
Violin	3 people

①   ②   ③   ④

18 대화를 듣고, 여자의 기분으로 알맞은 것을 고르시오.

① scared
② regretful
③ thrilled
④ tired

[19-20] 대화를 듣고, 여자의 마지막 말에 이어질 남자의 응답으로 가장 적절한 것을 고르시오.

19

① That's good to hear.
② They play classical music.
③ OK. I understand.
④ See you at 8 on Saturday.

20

① Oh, I'd love to go with you then.
② Dramas are my favorite.
③ OK. See you this Saturday.
④ Of course, I like action movies.

1 다음을 듣고, 그림을 가장 적절하게 묘사한 것을 고르시오.

① ② ③ ④

W ① They are watching a movie in a theater.
② They are taking pictures _____ _____ _____ _____ _____ .
③ They are _____ _____ _____ in a video shop.
④ They are _____ _____ _____ in an amusement park.

2 다음을 듣고, 남자가 어렸을 때 했던 일을 순서대로 나열한 것을 고르시오.

(A)　　　　(B)

(C)

① (A)-(B)-(C)
② (A)-(C)-(B)
③ (B)-(A)-(C)
④ (C)-(B)-(A)

M When I was a young child, my father _____ _____ _____ _____ to the park a lot. After he came home from work, _____ _____ _____ and then go to the park. It was _____ _____ _____ _____ . After we came home from the park, _____ _____ _____ _____ . Then I went to bed.

3 대화를 듣고, 어떤 상황에서 이루어지는 대화인지 고르시오.

① 음식 주문하기
② 음식 맛 평가하기
③ 맛있는 식당 추천하기
④ 수프 조리법 소개하기

M What kind of soup can I have _____ _____ _____ _____ ?
W Onion, tomato, or mushroom. But I recommend _____ _____ _____ . It's the best.
M No, I don't like mushroom soup.
W Well, _____ _____ _____ the tomato soup. It's delicious, too.
M OK. _____ _____ _____ . Thank you.

4 대화를 듣고, 남자가 주말에 한 일이 <u>아닌</u> 것을 고르시오.

① 채소 따기
② 음식 만들기
③ 시골에 가기
④ 채소밭일 돕기

M I visited my grandparents _____ _____ _____ last weekend.

W What did you do there?

M I worked outside. I helped my grandpa with his _____ _____ _____. And I picked some vegetables for grandma to cook.

W Sounds fun. You should _____ _____ _____ and help them.

M Can you come with me next time?

5 다음을 듣고, 무엇에 관한 안내인지 고르시오.

① 영어 회화 시험
② 교사와의 학업 상담
③ 담임선생님 연락처
④ 영어 작문 대회

M Good morning, students. This is Principal Grey speaking. _____ _____ _____ _____ an English essay writing contest. Essays can be _____ _____ _____. You must finish them and give them to your teacher by May 13th. _____ _____ _____, ask your homeroom teacher.

6 대화를 듣고, 여자의 장래희망으로 알맞은 것을 고르시오.

① scientist
② accountant
③ banker
④ math teacher

M What is your best subject?

W Math.

M That's great. _____ _____ _____ for many jobs. Scientists, bankers, for example, must be good at math.

W But I want to teach others. I like _____ _____ _____.

M And _____ _____ _____ _____?

W Yes, I do.

M Then it should be a good job for you.

7 다음을 듣고, 두 사람의 대화가 <u>어색한</u> 것을 고르시오.

①　　②　　③　　④

① **W** She's planning a surprise birthday party for her friend.
　 M Oh! _____ _____ _____!

② **W** I found your pencil under the desk. Here it is.
　 M Thank you very much.

③ **W** You didn't _____ _____ _____.
　 M Please _____ _____.

④ **W** My mother is very sick.
　 M I'm sorry to hear that.

8 대화를 듣고, 여자가 남자에게 전화를 건 목적을 고르시오.

① 버스 정류장의 위치를 물어보려고
② 버스의 출발 시간을 물어보려고
③ 버스 번호가 몇 번인지 물어보려고
④ 도착지까지의 소요시간을 물어보려고

[Telephone rings.]

M Hello. Central City Bus Station. How may I help you?

W Hello. I need to take a bus to Jonestown.

M Yes.

W How often do buses _____ _____ _____ for Jonestown?

M A bus for Jonestown leaves _____ _____ _____.

W What time?

M Ten minutes _____ _____ _____.

9 다음을 듣고, 남자에게 어울리는 속담으로 알맞은 것을 고르시오.

① All roads lead to Rome.
② When in Rome do as the Romans do.
③ A little knowledge is a dangerous thing.
④ Rome was not built in a day.

M I come from, but I have lived in Korea for 10 years. Last summer I met a Canadian man on the streets of Seoul. He wanted to _____ _____ _____, but I didn't shake his hand quickly. _____ _____ _____. I bent my head down. It was funny. I had learned to _____ _____ a Korean.

10 다음을 듣고, 여자가 여름에 하는 일이 아닌 것을 고르시오.

① 일광욕하기
② 수영하기
③ 아르바이트 하기
④ 바비큐 해먹기

W Summer is my favorite season. The weather is very hot, but I like _____ _____. I love to wear shorts and T-shirts and go to the beach. At the beach I can go swimming or _____ _____ _____ _____. I also like _____ _____ _____ in the summer. Barbecued chicken and hotdogs are delicious.

11 다음을 듣고, 무엇에 관한 설명인지 고르시오.

① ② ③ ④

M This building has _____ _____. Sometimes it can be very big. It can have 200 or more rooms. When a tourist or a _____ _____ _____ to a new city, he or she sleeps in a room in one of these. People _____ _____ _____ _____ here every night.

12 다음을 듣고, 이어폰으로 음악을 들을 때 주의해야 할 점으로 언급된 것을 고르시오.

① 소리를 작게 해서 듣기
② 다른 사람들에게 방해가 되지 않게 듣기
③ 한쪽으로 듣지 말고 양쪽으로 듣기
④ 좋은 이어폰으로 듣기

W Young people have _____ _____ these days. They listen to loud music on their MP3 players _____ _____ . The loud music hurts their ears. So _____ _____ _____ _____ on your MP3 player. If the volume is high, it might hurt your ears.

13 다음을 듣고, 주어진 상황에서 할 수 있는 말로 가장 적절한 것을 고르시오.

① Your father is proud of you.
② My father is very healthy.
③ Let me know if I can help.
④ Long time no see.

M Your best friend _____ _____ _____ one day. He says that his father is really sick. He says his father will have to _____ _____ _____ _____ for a long time. You become sad and _____ _____ _____ _____ . In this situation, what would you say to your friend?

14 다음을 듣고, 게시물의 내용과 일치하지 않는 것을 고르시오.

Rules for riding the roller coaster:
• Take off your backpack and hat before sitting down.
• Leave your hat and backpack at the entrance.
• Do not throw things to the ground while the coaster is going.
• Children under 120 cm tall are not allowed to ride it.

①   ②   ③   ④

W ① _____ _____ your hat and backpack before riding.
② You cannot ride with your _____ _____ _____ .
③ Do not _____ _____ from the roller coaster.
④ Children _____ _____ _____ old cannot ride the roller coaster.

15 대화를 듣고, Brian의 생일이 며칠 남았는지 고르시오.

① 7일
② 13일
③ 17일
④ 30일

M Brian's birthday is _____ _____ _____.

W Oh, is it? I thought it was next month.

M No, _____ _____ _____ _____ of this month. And it's the 13th today.

W So there are _____ _____ _____ _____ until his birthday.

M We have lots of time to buy a present. What will we buy for him?

16 대화를 듣고, 남자가 하는 말의 의도로 알맞은 것을 고르시오.

① 칭찬
② 권유
③ 질투
④ 명령

M I play the guitar. I love playing the guitar. What about you? Can you _____ _____ _____ _____?

W No, but I want to learn to play the guitar.

M You should take lessons. It's a lot of fun to _____ _____ _____.

W I think so, too.

M My teacher is great. He will help you a lot. _____ _____ _____ my teacher to you?

17 다음을 듣고, 도표의 내용과 일치하지 <u>않는</u> 것을 고르시오.

Musical Instruments which the students in Suji's class play.	
Piano	👤👤👤👤👤👤👤👤👤👤 10 people
Guitar	👤👤👤👤👤 5 people
Cello	👤👤👤 3 people
Violin	👤👤👤 3 people

① ② ③ ④

W ① More students play the piano _____ _____ _____.

② More students play the guitar than the violin.

③ _____ _____ _____ of students play the guitar and the cello.

④ Three students _____ _____ _____.

18 대화를 듣고, 여자의 기분으로 알맞은 것을 고르시오.

① scared
② regretful
③ thrilled
④ tired

M How was the ride?

W The ride? It was wonderful. Couldn't you _____ _____ _____ ?

M Everyone on the Viking was screaming.

W It feels like we're _____ _____ _____ _____ .

M It scares me.

W Not me. _____ _____ . I want to do it again.

19 대화를 듣고, 여자의 마지막 말에 이어질 남자의 응답으로 가장 적절한 것을 고르시오.

① That's good to hear.
② They play classical music.
③ OK. I understand.
④ See you at 8 on Saturday.

M Would you like to go to a concert with me on Saturday?

W _____ _____ ?

M It's *the Sky Boys*. You like them, _____ _____ ?

W Not really. I don't really like _____ _____ _____ _____ . I like classical music.

M So you don't want to come with me.

W No, _____ _____ .

M _____

20 대화를 듣고, 여자의 마지막 말에 이어질 남자의 응답으로 가장 적절한 것을 고르시오.

① Oh, I'd love to go with you then.
② Dramas are my favorite.
③ OK. See you this Saturday.
④ Of course, I like action movies.

W _____ _____ _____ _____ tomorrow? Let's go to a movie.

M What kind of movies do you like?

W _____ _____ .

M So do I. So is there a new romantic comedy you want to see?

W Yes, there is. Many people said _____ _____ is a great movie.

M _____

WORD AND EXPRESSION REVIEW • TEST 11-12

A Write down the definition of each word or phrase.

1 politely

2 considerate

3 speed limit

4 government

5 draw

6 physical education

7 greasy

8 appreciate

9 referee

10 irregular

11 theater

12 amusement park

13 daily

14 suggest

15 principal

16 announce

17 forgive

18 bow

19 behave

20 allow

B Match each word with the right definition.

1 pay for _____

2 penalty _____

3 tie _____

4 bend down _____

5 recommend _____

6 admit _____

7 agree _____

8 homeroom teacher _____

9 comfort _____

10 ticket _____

11 write down _____

12 treatment _____

13 behind _____

14 not much _____

15 seem _____

a 위로하다

b 동의하다.

c 천만에, 어림도 없어

d 위반 딱지

e ~에 대한 값을 지불하다

f 기재하다, 적다, 기록하다

g 입학을 허락하다

h ~인 것 같다, ~인 듯하다

i ~의 뒤에

j 취급, 대우, 치료

k ~와 동점이 되다

l 벌칙, 벌금

m 추천하다, 권하다

n 담임선생님

o 아래로 구부리다, 숙이다

C Choose the best answer for the blank.

1 Could you _____ me a favor?

    a. do   b. give   c. take

2 Why was she absent _____ school yesterday?

    a. of   b. to   c. from

3 I want to shake _____ with him.

    a. hand   b. a hand   c. hands

4 I can carry the boxes with _____ .

    a. ease   b. easy   c. easily

5 It is foolish of him to _____ such a mistake.

    a. do   b. have   c. make

6 When I was young, I _____ often take a walk after lunch.

    a. would   b. should   c. might

D Complete the short dialogues.

1 A: How often do you drink alcohol?

    B: I _____ to drink while young, but I don't drink now.

2 A: I like classical music more than popular music.

    B: So _____ _____ .

3 A: Tom's birthday is on the 20th.

    B: So there are 5 days to _____ until his birthday.

4 A: You didn't _____ your promise.

    B: Please forgive me.

5 A: Can you drive?

    B: No, I don't know _____ to drive.

1 다음을 듣고, 피자를 먹은 후 바로 다음에 한 일을 고르시오.

① eating ice cream
② taking a bus
③ playing at the park
④ buying presents

2 대화를 듣고, 여자의 직업으로 알맞은 것을 고르시오.

① pilot
② bus driver
③ taxi driver
④ flight attendant

3 다음을 듣고, 주어진 상황에서 할 수 있는 말로 알맞은 것을 고르시오.

① Can I have one?
② You are very strong.
③ I'll get the door for you.
④ Can you open this door?

4 대화를 듣고, 여자가 머리를 짧게 자른 이유를 고르시오.

① 친구들의 권유로
② 긴 머리가 싫증나서
③ 날씨가 너무 더워서
④ 친구의 짧은 머리가 예뻐 보여서

5 대화를 듣고, 두 사람이 만날 장소를 고르시오.

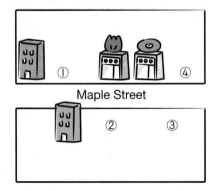

6 대화를 듣고, 남자가 살 것이 <u>아닌</u> 것을 고르시오.

① 바지
② 넥타이
③ 스웨터
④ 셔츠

7 대화를 듣고, 여자가 전화를 한 목적을 고르시오.

① 차를 빼달라고
② 차를 견인하겠다고
③ 주문한 차가 들어왔다고
④ 도난 차량 신고를 하려고

8 대화를 듣고, 남자가 이용할 교통수단을 고르시오.

① 버스
② 택시
③ 자동차
④ 지하철

9 대화를 듣고, 남자가 주말에 한 일을 고르시오.

① 태국 여행
② 군대 간 아들 면회
③ 잃어버린 아들 찾기
④ 공항에 부모님 마중 나가기

10 다음을 듣고, 두 사람의 대화가 <u>어색한</u> 것을 고르시오.

①   ②   ③   ④

11 대화를 듣고, 여자가 지불해야 할 금액을 고르시오.

<Museum of Ancient Korean History>

Adults	5,000 won
Children/Teens (6~18 years old)	2,000 won
Seniors (65 years and older)	free
Group of 10 or more	20% discount

① 10,000 won
② 12,000 won
③ 14,000 won
④ 16,000 won

12 대화를 듣고, 여자가 지불해야 할 금액을 고르시오.

① 7,000 won
② 7,700 won
③ 8,000 won
④ 8,400 won

13 대화를 듣고, 남자의 심정으로 알맞은 것을 고르시오.

① angry
② happy
③ worried
④ disappointed

14 다음을 듣고, 환경오염을 줄이는 방법으로 여자가 주장하는 것을 고르시오.

① 자전거 타기
② 소형차 운전하기
③ 대중교통 이용하기
④ 무공해 자동차 개발하기

15 대화를 듣고, 남자가 하는 말의 의도로 알맞은 것을 고르시오.

① 명령
② 칭찬
③ 권유
④ 의논

16 다음을 듣고, 그림의 상황에 가장 알맞은 대화를 고르시오.

①   ②   ③   ④

17 대화를 듣고, 두 사람의 관계로 알맞은 것을 고르시오.

① 학생 – 교수
② 점원 – 손님
③ 면접관 – 구직자
④ 취재기자 – 운동선수

18 대화를 듣고, 내용과 일치하지 <u>않는</u> 것을 고르시오.

① 여자는 공원에서 산책을 했다.
② 남자는 일요일에 공원에 갔다.
③ 여자는 토요일에 공원에 갔다.
④ 남자는 공원에서 인라인 스케이트를 탔다.

[19-20] 대화를 듣고, 여자의 마지막 말에 이어질 남자의 응답으로 가장 적절한 것을 고르시오.

19

① I'll be right back.
② I can do it by myself.
③ I don't need a refill.
④ Sugar is bad for you.

20

① Where do I buy it?
② Cheer up. It's not too bad.
③ Thanks. I really appreciate it.
④ Why don't you use the cleanser cream?

TEST

13

1 다음을 듣고, 피자를 먹은 후 바로 다음에 한 일을 고르시오.

① eating ice cream
② taking a bus
③ playing at the park
④ buying presents

W I had _____ _____ _____ _____ on the weekend. My mom took my friends and me to a pizza restaurant. We ate a lot of food, then we all went to _____ _____ _____. After playing at the park, we went to an ice cream shop and ate ice cream. _____ _____ _____ lots of presents.

2 대화를 듣고, 여자의 직업으로 알맞은 것을 고르시오.

① pilot
② bus driver
③ taxi driver
④ flight attendant

W Please fasten your seat belt, sir. The plane _____ _____ _____ in 20 minutes and the seat belt _____ _____ _____.
M OK. I will. By the way, would you tell me how long it will take _____ _____ _____ to the nearest city?
W About 30 minutes by taxi. You can easily find a place to stay.
M Good. Thank you.

3 다음을 듣고, 주어진 상황에서 할 수 있는 말로 알맞은 것을 고르시오.

① Can I have one?
② You are very strong.
③ I'll get the door for you.
④ Can you open this door?

M You are standing near the door of an office building. A woman is _____ _____ _____ _____. She is carrying two boxes, so she cannot open the door. You want to _____ _____ _____ _____ the door open. In this situation, what would you say to the woman?

4 대화를 듣고, 여자가 머리를 짧게 자른 이유를 고르시오.

① 친구들의 권유로
② 긴 머리가 싫증나서
③ 날씨가 너무 더워서
④ 친구의 짧은 머리가 예뻐 보여서

M Hi, Sumin. It's hot today. Oh, you got your hair cut. Your hair was long for a long time.
W Yes, I got _____ _____ _____ _____ last week.
M It looks nice.
W Really? My friends said _____ _____ _____ _____ with short hair. I thought _____ _____ _____ _____.
M So you got your hair cut.
W That's right.

5 대화를 듣고, 두 사람이 만날 장소를 고르시오.

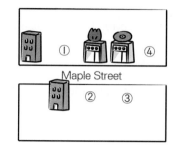

W Let's meet at a cafe on Maple Street.

M Where is the cafe?

W The cafe is _____ _____ _____ and a DVD shop on Maple Street.

M But there are two banks on Maple Street.

W You're right. Well, do you know the flower shop there? The cafe is _____ _____ _____ _____ .

M OK. I got it. It's near a bank and a DVD shop and it's opposite the flower shop _____ _____ _____ _____ , right?

W Right. I'll meet you at 2 p.m.

M See you then.

6 대화를 듣고, 남자가 살 것이 <u>아닌</u> 것을 고르시오.

① 바지
② 넥타이
③ 스웨터
④ 셔츠

M I need to go to the clothes shop.

W What do you need? A sweater?

M No, I have many sweaters. _____ _____ _____ and I've lost some weight.

W Are your pants too big?

M That's right. I need some new pants.

W Do you want me to go with you? I have a _____ _____ _____ of fashion than you. And a lot of your clothes are old. You should buy _____ _____ _____ _____ , too.

M I think so. I'd appreciate _____ _____ _____ with me.

7 대화를 듣고, 여자가 전화를 한 목적을 고르시오.

① 차를 빼달라고
② 차를 견인하겠다고
③ 주문한 차가 들어왔다고
④ 도난 차량 신고를 하려고

[Telephone rings.]

M Hello.

W Hello. _____ _____ _____ a white Sonata?

M Yes. What's wrong?

W Is it _____ _____ _____ _____ GG apartments?

M Yes. I'm at my friend's house.

W Sir. It's in front of my car. _____ _____ _____ my car.

M Oh, I'm sorry. I will move my car now.

W Please hurry and move your car. I am late.

8 대화를 듣고, 남자가 이용할 교통수단을 고르시오.

① 버스
② 택시
③ 자동차
④ 지하철

M How long does it take to Seoul Station by subway?

W About 45 minutes.

M And _____ _____ _____ _____?

W Not really. Right now traffic will be bad. I think you should _____ _____ _____.

M I am too tired to take a subway.

W But it'll _____ _____ _____ by bus or taxi.

M OK. I see.

9 대화를 듣고, 남자가 주말에 한 일을 고르시오.

① 태국 여행
② 군대 간 아들 면회
③ 잃어버린 아들 찾기
④ 공항에 부모님 마중 나가기

W Did you have a good weekend?

M I had _____ _____ _____.

W Why was that?

M My son _____ _____ at the airport. He ran off to look at _____ _____ _____.

W Oh, no.

M It took me one hour to find him. I was really worried.

W Why were you at the airport? Did you take a weekend trip?

M No, _____ _____ _____ my mom and dad. They flew to Thailand for a vacation.

10 다음을 듣고, 두 사람의 대화가 <u>어색한</u> 것을 고르시오.

①　　②　　③　　④

① **W** I played computer games _____ _____ _____ last night.

　M How long did you play?

② **W** Do you like Korean food?

　M Yes, _____ _____ _____. I love it.

③ **W** _____ _____ _____. I'm going to the baseball game tonight.

　M The Lions beat the Unicorns 7 to 3.

④ **W** How long does it take to do that?

　M It takes about 10 minutes. Would you _____ _____ _____ _____ here?

11 대화를 듣고, 여자가 지불해야 할 금액을 고르시오.

〈Museum of Ancient Korean History〉

Adults	5,000 won
Children/Teens (6~18 years old)	2,000 won
Seniors (65 years and older)	free
Group of 10 or more	20% discount

① 10,000 won
② 12,000 won
③ 14,000 won
④ 16,000 won

M How many tickets do you need, ma'am?

W Let's see. There are my husband and I.

M _____ _____ _____.

W And our three children.

M How old is _____ _____?

W 5 years old. The oldest is 10, and the next is 8 years old.

M Then _____ _____ _____ _____ children's tickets.

12 대화를 듣고, 여자가 지불해야 할 금액을 고르시오.

① 7,000 won
② 7,700 won
③ 8,000 won
④ 8,400 won

M These donuts are very delicious. How much are these?

W They are 700 won each. Or you can buy 12 for 7,000 won.

M You mean if I buy 10, I can _____ _____ _____ _____.

W _____ _____ _____.

M Sounds good. I'll buy 12 then.

W _____ _____ _____ and put the donuts you'd like to have.

13 대화를 듣고, 남자의 심정으로 알맞은 것을 고르시오.

① angry
② happy
③ worried
④ disappointed

M Are you sure?

W Yes, I am sure. I heard Mom and Dad talking.

M And Dad wasn't angry with my mistakes?

W No, he wasn't. I guess he forgave you _____ _____ _____ _____.

M So they said they were going to _____ _____ _____ _____ _____ for my birthday. That's great. I'm so excited.

W Now you won't _____ _____ _____ _____ without a cell phone in your class.

14 다음을 듣고, 환경오염을 줄이는 방법으로 여자가 주장하는 것을 고르시오.

① 자전거 타기
② 소형차 운전하기
③ 대중교통 이용하기
④ 무공해 자동차 개발하기

W Pollution is a big problem _____ _____. Why does everyone want a bigger car? Bigger cars burn more gasoline and _____ _____ _____. We all should drive smaller cars. It would be great that all people take buses or the subway, but it is not possible. So that is not the answer. People must _____ _____ _____.

15 대화를 듣고, 남자가 하는 말의 의도로 알 맞은 것을 고르시오.

① 명령
② 칭찬
③ 권유
④ 의논

M You should _____ _____ in school.
W But I want to study history.
M If you study history, you can't go to medical school.
W Dad, you said _____ _____ _____.
M That's right. _____ _____ _____ _____. As you know, I'm a _____ _____, so I could help you a lot.

16 다음을 듣고, 그림의 상황에 가장 알맞은 대화를 고르시오.

① ② ③ ④

① **M** Will they come to my home and _____ _____ _____?
W Yes, they will. Please tell them our home address and phone number.
② **M** _____ _____ _____, otherwise we'll be late!
W We don't need to rush. The movie will start at 8:00 p.m.
③ **M** How come _____ _____ _____?
W _____ _____ _____ in the rain while coming back from the library.
④ **M** Would you be going to the post office, by any chance?
W No. But _____ _____ _____ _____ because it's on my way home. Do you need something?

17 대화를 듣고, 두 사람의 관계로 알맞은 것을 고르시오.

① 학생 – 교수
② 점원 – 손님
③ 면접관 – 구직자
④ 취재기자 – 운동선수

M Can you tell me _____ _____ _____?
W I graduated from A-1 University last year. I majored in business management.
M And do you have _____ _____ _____?
W No, I'm looking for _____ _____ _____. I don't have experience but I'll work very hard. I'd really appreciate it if I could work for you.

18 대화를 듣고, 내용과 일치하지 <u>않는</u> 것을 고르시오.

① 여자는 공원에서 산책을 했다.
② 남자는 일요일에 공원에 갔다.
③ 여자는 토요일에 공원에 갔다.
④ 남자는 공원에서 인라인 스케이트를 탔다.

M Did you go to the park last Sunday? You told me _____ _____.

W No. As I had to visit my uncle with my parents, I went to the park on Saturday. I _____ _____ _____ around the park.

M That's why _____ _____ _____ _____.

W You went to the park _____ _____?

M Yes, I did. I went in-line skating with my brother. I waited for you.

---

19 대화를 듣고, 여자의 마지막 말에 이어질 남자의 응답으로 가장 적절한 것을 고르시오.

① I'll be right back.
② I can do it by myself.
③ I don't need a refill.
④ Sugar is bad for you.

W That chocolate cake was _____ _____ _____. It was delicious.

M I'm glad you enjoyed it. Do you need anything else, ma'am?

W Could I please have some more coffee?

M OK. _____ _____ _____ _____ with your coffee.

W And I need some sugar. _____ _____ _____ _____ on the table.

M _____

---

20 대화를 듣고, 여자의 마지막 말에 이어질 남자의 응답으로 가장 적절한 것을 고르시오.

① Where do I buy it?
② Cheer up. It's not too bad.
③ Thanks. I really appreciate it.
④ Why don't you use the cleanser cream?

M Jenny, I need your help.

W What is it?

M My skin is not clear. I have _____ _____ _____.

W _____ _____ _____ in young people. Don't worry.

M But I'd like to have clear skin. What should I do?

W Choose a good _____ _____ _____ and your face will look and feel a lot better. Oh, I'll give you _____ _____ _____ tomorrow.

M _____

1 다음을 듣고, 그림의 상황에 가장 알맞은 대화를 고르시오.

① ② ③ ④

2 다음을 듣고, 어떤 계절에 관한 설명인지 고르시오.
① spring
② summer
③ fall
④ winter

3 대화를 듣고, 남자가 지금 할 일을 고르시오.
① to have lunch
② to get lunch ready
③ to go buy some snacks
④ to wait for the lunch time

4 대화를 듣고, 여자가 주말에 할 일로 일치하지 <u>않는</u> 것을 고르시오.
① 토요일에는 도서관에 가서 책을 반납한다.
② 토요일에는 과학숙제를 한다.
③ 일요일에는 가족과 공원에 간다.
④ 일요일에는 가족과 식당에서 저녁을 먹는다.

5 대화를 듣고, 엄마가 만든 것을 고르시오.
① 오렌지 주스
② 샌드위치
③ 토마토 주스
④ 스파게티

6 대화를 듣고, 두 사람이 현재 있는 장소를 고르시오.
① 교실 ② 운동장
③ 교무실 ④ 문방구점

7 다음을 듣고, 두 사람의 대화가 <u>어색한</u> 것을 고르시오.
① ② ③ ④

8 대화를 듣고, 내용에 가장 알맞은 안내문을 고르시오.
① NO STUDENT DISCOUNT!
② YOU MAY NOT CANCEL THE TICKET!
③ ADULTS ONLY!
④ THE TICKETS ARE SOLD OUT!

9 대화를 듣고, 여자의 장래희망을 고르시오.
① builder
② architect
③ painter
④ interior designer

10 대화를 듣고, 여자가 말하고자 하는 속담으로 알맞은 것을 고르시오.
① A little pot is soon hot.
② A watched pot never boils.
③ Pot calls the kettle black.
④ Clothes make the man.

11 다음을 듣고, 무엇에 관한 내용인지 고르시오.
①

②

③

④

12 대화를 듣고, 여자가 전화를 건 목적으로 알맞은 것을 고르시오.

① 같이 공부하려고
② 고민을 상담하려고
③ 수학 시험을 도와주려고
④ 수학 시험 범위를 물어보려고

13 대화를 듣고, 남자의 증상으로 알맞은 것을 고르시오.

① 감기
② 치통
③ 두통
④ 불면증

14 대화를 듣고, 여자가 결국 하게 된 것을 고르시오.

① 주문
② 교환
③ 환불
④ 불평

15 대화를 듣고, 남자가 있는 곳의 현재 시각을 고르시오.

① 10:00 a.m.
② 2:00 p.m.
③ 4:00 p.m.
④ 10:00 p.m.

16 대화를 듣고, 여자의 심경으로 알맞은 것을 고르시오.

① thankful
② worried
③ apologetic
④ angry

17 다음을 듣고, 이어지는 질문에 어울리는 대답을 고르시오.

① They buy their mother flowers.
② They give their mother small gifts.
③ They give money to their mother.
④ They make some food for their mother.

18 다음을 듣고, 요일별 날씨가 바르게 연결된 것을 고르시오.

① Saturday - sunny
② Sunday - cloudy
③ Monday - stormy
④ Tuesday - rainy

[19~20] 대화를 듣고, 여자의 마지막 말에 이어질 남자의 응답으로 가장 적절한 것을 고르시오.

19

① Orange and apple.
② I really like grapes.
③ Chocolate. Chocolate milk.
④ Some more juice, please.

20

① OK. I'll eat at home then.
② Help yourself. Enjoy the food.
③ OK. That's a good time for me.
④ Hurry or you'll be late.

TEST

14

1 다음을 듣고, 그림의 상황에 가장 알맞은 대화를 고르시오.

① ② ③ ④

① **M** I'm really sorry for making you wait so long.

  W It's OK. Did you _____ _____ in a traffic jam?

② **M** How may I help you today?

  W I need to change my appointment.

③ **M** When is _____ _____ _____ _____ _____ for you?

  W Anytime on Tuesday is fine.

④ **M** Thank you for coming to my place.

  W _____ _____ _____.

2 다음을 듣고, 어떤 계절에 관한 설명인지 고르시오.

① spring
② summer
③ fall
④ winter

W In this season, the weather _____ _____ _____ _____. Before the snow comes, the leaves on the trees _____ _____, orange and brown and _____ _____. The days can be hot and sunny, but the nights are cool.

3 대화를 듣고, 남자가 지금 할 일을 고르시오.

① to have lunch
② to get lunch ready
③ to go buy some snacks
④ to wait for the lunch time

M Is it time for lunch?

W _____, _____ _____. It's only 11.

M But I'm really hungry, Mom.

W You'll have to wait. I'll _____ _____ _____ in an hour.

M I can't wait. Are there _____ _____?

W No. _____ _____ _____ _____ last night.

M I'll go to the convenience store and buy something.

W OK. If you're really hungry!

4 대화를 듣고, 여자가 주말에 할 일로 일치하지 <u>않는</u> 것을 고르시오.

① 토요일에는 도서관에 책을 반납한다.
② 토요일에는 과학숙제를 한다.
③ 일요일에는 가족과 공원에 간다.
④ 일요일에는 가족과 식당에서 저녁을 먹는다.

M What are you going to do this weekend?

W I will go to the library on Saturday.

M Do you _____ _____ _____?

W Yes, I need a science book. Then I'll _____ _____ _____ _____. I have to hand it in next Monday.

M And on Sunday?

W I will go to the park _____ _____ _____. Then we will have dinner in a restaurant.

5 대화를 듣고, 엄마가 만든 것을 고르시오.

① 오렌지 주스
② 샌드위치
③ 토마토 주스
④ 스파게티

M Mom, this is delicious. You're a _____ _____.

W Umm... What are you eating?

M _____ _____ _____.

W I didn't make the sandwich. _____ _____ _____. I made the tomato juice.

M It's good, too. Where is grandma? I'll tell grandma I liked her sandwich.

W _____ _____.

6 대화를 듣고, 두 사람이 현재 있는 장소를 고르시오.

① 교실
② 운동장
③ 교무실
④ 문방구점

M I'll _____ _____ _____.

W Does the teacher need any more chalk?

M No, there is _____ _____ _____.

W That's good. After you clean the blackboard, I'll go outside and _____ _____ _____.

M Good idea. The teacher will be here, soon.

7 다음을 듣고, 두 사람의 대화가 <u>어색한</u> 것을 고르시오.

①   ②   ③   ④

① **M** What is your father's job?
   W He is an English teacher in a high school.

② **M** You look tired. Are you feeling OK?
   W No, I _____ _____ _____ all day long.

③ **M** _____ _____ _____ tonight.
   W OK. I'll cook spaghetti.

④ **M** I must get up early tomorrow.
   W You should _____ _____ _____ _____.

8 대화를 듣고, 내용에 가장 알맞은 안내문을 고르시오.

① NO STUDENT DISCOUNT!
② YOU MAY NOT CANCEL THE TICKET!
③ ADULTS ONLY!
④ THE TICKETS ARE SOLD OUT!

W I can't go to the concert that I have hoped to see _____ _____ _____.

M Why not? Your dad won't _____ _____ _____.

W No, my dad said it was OK. The tickets are sold out.

M There are _____ _____ _____. That's too bad. You _____ _____ _____ but to go to the next concert.

W Oh, no. I can't wait to go to the next concert.

9 대화를 듣고, 여자의 장래희망을 고르시오.

① builder
② architect
③ painter
④ interior designer

M The buildings all look the same. _____ _____, _____ _____. What do you think of it?

W You can say that again. It's too boring. I want to change that.

M Do you want to build buildings in the future?

W No, I want to _____ _____.

M Oh, you might be good at that. _____ _____ _____.

W Thank you. I want to design some new apartment buildings.

10 대화를 듣고, 여자가 말하고자 하는 속담으로 알맞은 것을 고르시오.

① A little pot is soon hot.
② A watched pot never boils.
③ Pot calls the kettle black.
④ Clothes make the man.

W I'm worried about the homework.

M You didn't do your homework.

W _____, _____ _____. I was very busy yesterday.

M That's not good. The teacher will be angry.

W John, _____ _____ _____ like that. Yesterday you didn't do your homework. And _____ _____ _____ _____ you didn't do your homework, too.

M You're right. I can't say you're bad because I do it, too.

W You are _____ _____ _____ _____ in that famous English saying.

11 다음을 듣고, 무엇에 관한 내용인지 고르시오.

① ② ③ ④

M This is usually _____ _____ _____ _____ children have. They can ride one when they are three years old. It has _____ _____ _____ in the front and two smaller wheels _____ _____ _____. Young children sit on a seat and _____ _____ _____ _____.

12 대화를 듣고, 여자가 전화를 건 목적으로 알맞은 것을 고르시오.

① 같이 공부하려고
② 고민을 상담하려고
③ 수학 시험을 도와주려고
④ 수학 시험 범위를 물어보려고

[Telephone rings.]

M Hello.

W Hello, Minsu. It's Jihye. I need your help.

M How can I help you?

W It's the math test tomorrow. I am having troubles _____ _____ _____.

M Do you want to _____ _____ _____ ?

W Yes, I do. I hope you can _____ _____ _____ _____.

M Come on over to my house.

13 대화를 듣고, 남자의 증상으로 알맞은 것을 고르시오.

① 감기
② 치통
③ 두통
④ 불면증

W You look sick. Do you have a cold?

M No, I don't have a cold.

W _____ _____ ?

M No, it's one of my teeth. _____ _____ _____. I couldn't sleep a wink last night.

W Why don't you go see a doctor? _____ _____ is very good. You can see him.

M OK. Thank you.

14 대화를 듣고, 여자가 결국 하게 된 것을 고르시오.

① 주문
② 교환
③ 환불
④ 불평

W _____ _____.

M May I help you?

W This shirt is too big. I bought it for my father yesterday.

M Would you like _____ _____ _____?

W Yes, I would.

M Let me check. *[pause]* I'm sorry, but I don't have any smaller sizes.

W Oh, that's too bad. Can I _____ _____ _____ _____, then?

M Yes, you can. Do you _____ _____ _____?

15 대화를 듣고, 남자가 있는 곳의 현재 시각을 고르시오.

① 10:00 a.m.
② 2:00 p.m.
③ 4:00 p.m.
④ 10:00 p.m.

[Cell phone rings.]

M Hello.

W Hi, Dad, this is Susan.

M _____ _____ _____ from you, Susan. What time is it in Korea?

W 2 o'clock in the afternoon. I'm _____ _____ _____ of you. Are you at home now?

M You're right. I'm home. Do you want to speak to your mom?

W Oh, yes. I _____ _____ _____ _____ very much, Mom and Dad.

16 대화를 듣고, 여자의 심경으로 알맞은 것을 고르시오.

① thankful
② worried
③ apologetic
④ angry

M Did you bring my book?

W Your book? What do you mean?

M Don't you remember _____ _____ _____ _____ _____ last week?

W Oh, no. I'm sorry. You told me to bring it back, but I forgot.

M That's too bad. I was going to read it today.

W _____ _____. It's my mistake. Should I go home and get it?

M No, but please _____ _____ _____ it tomorrow.

17 다음을 듣고, 이어지는 질문에 어울리는 대답을 고르시오.

① They buy their mother flowers.
② They give their mother small gifts.
③ They give money to their mother.
④ They make some food for their mother.

M In Korea people _____ _____ _____. They buy their parents flowers or _____ _____ _____. But in America there are Mother's Day and Father's Day. In America the children _____ _____ _____ for their parents. For example, they clean the house or _____ _____ on Mother's Day.

Q What do American children do on Mother's Day?

18 다음을 듣고, 요일별 날씨가 바르게 연결된 것을 고르시오.

① Saturday – sunny
② Sunday – cloudy
③ Monday – stormy
④ Tuesday – rainy

M Good Saturday evening, nightly news listeners. I'm J. J. Jones. A storm is coming. It will be a very _____ _____. You should bring inside things that can _____ _____ tomorrow morning. You must _____ _____ _____. The storm will last for two days. On Tuesday it will be cloudy. The storm will be over.

19 대화를 듣고, 여자의 마지막 말에 이어질 남자의 응답으로 가장 적절한 것을 고르시오.

① Orange and apple.
② I really like grapes.
③ Chocolate. Chocolate milk.
④ Some more juice, please.

M May I have your order, please?
W I'm waiting for my friends. But _____ _____ _____.
M Would you like something to drink first?
W What do you have?
M We have _____ _____ _____.
W _____ _____ _____ juice do you have?
M _____

20 대화를 듣고, 여자의 마지막 말에 이어질 남자의 응답으로 가장 적절한 것을 고르시오.

① OK. I'll eat at home then.
② Help yourself. Enjoy the food.
③ OK. That's a good time for me.
④ Hurry or you'll be late.

W _____ _____ _____ _____ at 5 o'clock?
M No, that's too early.
W I wanted to _____ _____ _____ _____.
M But I have to finish my homework before I meet you.
W OK. Let's meet at 7 in front of the theater.
M That's fine. Is there _____ _____ _____ before the movie?
W No, there isn't. The movie starts at 7:15.
M _____

Ⓐ Write down the definition of each word or phrase.

1	opposite	11	facial
2	ancient	12	traffic jam
3	tray	13	appointment
4	pollute	14	cancel
5	environment	15	creative
6	surgeon	16	pot
7	rush	17	explain
8	business management	18	apologize
9	look for	19	celebrate
10	common	20	protect

Ⓑ Match each word with the right definition.

1	own (v.)	a	착륙하다, 도착하다
2	biology	b	~을 향해, ~쪽으로
3	pimple	c	소유하다
4	blow away	d	길을 잃다, 미아가 되다
5	get lost	e	(사람, 짐 등을) 차에서 도중에 내려놓다
6	thirsty	f	생물
7	wheel	g	풀다, 해결하다
8	last (v.)	h	뾰루지, 여드름
9	toward	i	편리한, 편한
10	drop off	j	매진되다, 품절되다
11	convenient	k	탈것, 차, 운송수단
12	vehicle	l	바퀴
13	be sold out	m	날리다, 날아가다, 흩날리다
14	land (v.)	n	계속되다, 지속하다
15	resolve	o	목마른

C Choose the best answer for the blank.

1 I have no choice _____ to go to the next concert.

  a. but b. without c. except

2 He graduated _____ a medical school.

  a. of b. as c. from

3 Did you get _____ in a traffic jam?

  a. met b. caught c. kept

4 Thank you for _____ the door open.

  a. giving b. holding c. trying

5 What did you major _____ at college?

  a. in b. by c. with

6 Would you like something _____ drink?

  a. of b. for c. to

D Complete the short dialogues.

1 A: It's cold outside tonight.

  B: You can _____ that again. I can't wait until summer arrives.

2 A: Do you have a cold?

  B: No, I have a toothache. I couldn't sleep a _____ last night.

3 A: You look different today.

  B: I _____ my hair cut short.

4 A: Do you have the bus timetable by any _____?

  B: Yes, here it is.

5 A: How much is it?

  B: You don't have to pay for it. I'll fix it _____ free.

1 다음을 듣고, 상황에 맞는 그림을 고르시오.

① 　②

③ 　④

2 다음을 듣고, 남자에 대한 설명으로 옳은 것을 고르시오.

① 걸어서 살을 뺐다.
② 현재 몸무게는 70kg이다.
③ 헬스클럽에서 운동을 했다.
④ 고기 대신 야채를 많이 먹는다.

3 대화를 듣고, 남자가 아침식사로 먹지 <u>않는</u> 것을 고르시오.

① 시리얼
② 사과
③ 토스트
④ 우유

4 대화를 듣고, 남자와 여자가 선호하는 공부 장소로 바르게 짝지어진 것을 고르시오.

　　〈남자〉　〈여자〉
① 집　　— 학교
② 도서관 — 집
③ 집　　— 도서관
④ 학교　— 도서관

5 대화를 듣고, 남자의 직업으로 알맞은 것을 고르시오.

① bus driver
② taxi driver
③ teacher
④ ticket agent

6 다음을 듣고, 여자가 주장하는 것으로 알맞은 것을 고르시오.

① 교육적인 방송을 늘려야 한다.
② 경찰 드라마를 더 많이 제작해야 한다.
③ 경찰 드라마는 사실에 바탕을 두어야 한다.
④ 어린이 프로그램에서 폭력적인 장면을 없애야 한다.

7 대화를 듣고, 여자가 싫어하는 동물을 고르시오.

8 대화를 듣고, 남자가 잊고 온 것을 고르시오.

① bag
② umbrella
③ textbook
④ homework

9 대화를 듣고, 남자가 새 바지를 사려고 하는 이유를 고르시오.

① 바지가 낡아서
② 축구복이 필요해서
③ 바지에 구멍이 나서
④ 바지의 얼룩이 지워지지 않아서

10 대화를 듣고, 남자가 <u>잘못</u> 누른 전화번호의 개수를 고르시오.

① 1개　　② 2개　　③ 3개　　④ 4개

11 다음을 듣고, 표의 내용과 일치하지 <u>않는</u> 것을 고르시오.

Name	Number of brothers	Number of sisters
Jinho	0	0
Sanghyun	1	0
Mihyun	1	2

① ② ③ ④

12 다음을 듣고, 두 사람의 대화가 <u>어색한</u> 것을 고르시오.

① ② ③ ④

13 대화를 듣고, 남자가 지불해야 될 금액을 고르시오.

① $120
② $140
③ $160
④ $200

14 대화를 듣고, 대화가 이루어지는 장소를 고르시오.

① dentist's
② pharmacy
③ candy store
④ emergency room

15 대화를 듣고, 무엇에 관한 내용인지 고르시오.

① 분실물 신고하기
② 선물 품목 정하기
③ 생일 파티 장소 정하기
④ 옷에 어울리는 시계 고르기

16 다음을 듣고, 주어진 상황에서 할 수 있는 말로 가장 적절한 것을 고르시오.

① It's nice to meet you.
② I want to meet you.
③ Please introduce me.
④ What do you think about me?

17 다음을 듣고, 그림의 상황에 가장 알맞은 대화를 고르시오.

① ② ③ ④

18 대화를 듣고, 여자의 심경으로 가장 알맞은 것을 고르시오.

① annoyed
② excited
③ scared
④ brave

[19-20] 대화를 듣고, 남자의 마지막 말에 이어질 여자의 응답으로 가장 적절한 것을 고르시오.

19

① She is doing well.
② She is right over there.
③ She needs a new sweater.
④ My older sister is 18 years old.

20

① Cook it medium-rare, please.
② Onion soup or vegetable soup.
③ Onion soup is my favorite.
④ Meat sauce spaghetti.

1 다음을 듣고, 상황에 맞는 그림을 고르시오.

① ② ③ ④

W Last night I ate dinner at my friend's house. _____ _____ _____ _____, I read comic books with my friend _____ _____ _____ _____. My friend's sister _____ _____ _____ on the table. And my friend's father was reading a newspaper.

2 다음을 듣고, 남자에 대한 설명으로 옳은 것을 고르시오.

① 걸어서 살을 뺐다.
② 현재 몸무게는 70kg이다.
③ 헬스클럽에서 운동을 했다.
④ 고기 대신 야채를 많이 먹는다.

M Four months ago, I weighed 80kg. Now I weigh 75kg. I am happy to _____ _____. I didn't play sports or go to the fitness center. Nor did I eat lots of vegetables. What did I do? I stopped driving _____ _____ _____ _____. I walk to the store now. And I _____ _____ _____ _____ in my office building and my apartment. Small changes can make a big difference.

3 대화를 듣고, 남자가 아침식사로 먹지 않는 것을 고르시오.

① 시리얼
② 사과
③ 토스트
④ 우유

M I'm so hungry. I'd like to have some snacks before lunch.
W Didn't you _____ _____ today?
M No, there wasn't any cereal or an apple.
W Cereal? You could eat rice or _____ _____ _____.
M I only eat cereal for breakfast _____ _____, and sometimes an apple.
W You'd better have more food. Eating breakfast is very important _____ _____ _____ and the body.

4 대화를 듣고, 남자와 여자가 선호하는 공부 장소로 바르게 짝지어진 것을 고르시오.

〈남자〉 〈여자〉
① 집 　 － 학교
② 도서관 － 집
③ 집 　 － 도서관
④ 학교 － 도서관

W Where do you usually study?
M I like to _____ _____ _____ in my room.
W _____ _____. I like to study at the library.
M My house is _____ _____ _____ to study. I can get food and have a drink.
W But when I study at home, I always start to watch TV.
M Not me. There is _____ _____ _____ in my room.

5 대화를 듣고, 남자의 직업으로 알맞은 것을 고르시오.

① bus driver
② taxi driver
③ teacher
④ ticket agent

W Excuse me, _____ _____ _____ _____ Cedarwood Middle School?
M No, I don't. You need the No.34 bus.
W Right here? At the _____ _____ _____?
M Yes. _____ _____ _____. A No.34 bus will be here soon.
W Great. Thank you very much.

6 다음을 듣고, 여자가 주장하는 것으로 알맞은 것을 고르시오.

① 교육적인 방송을 늘려야 한다.
② 경찰 드라마를 더 많이 제작해야 한다.
③ 경찰 드라마는 사실에 바탕을 두어야 한다.
④ 어린이 프로그램에서 폭력적인 장면을 없애야 한다.

W Why are there so many police dramas on TV? Guns, _____ _____ _____! TV has too _____ _____. There is too much death and fighting. We want to fight when we watch all this fighting. TV should teach us right things. TV should be _____ _____.

7 대화를 듣고, 여자가 싫어하는 동물을 고르시오.

① ② ③ ④

W I hate this animal.
M What is it?
W _____ _____ _____. It's long and thin.
M Does it have legs?
W No, it doesn't. It moves _____ _____ _____ _____ when it moves across the grass.
M Some of them _____ _____, and they have a long tongue, right?
W Yes, it does.

8 대화를 듣고, 남자가 잊고 온 것을 고르시오.

① bag
② umbrella
③ textbook
④ homework

M Oh, no!

W _____ _____?

M I forgot something at home.

W What is it? Your homework or a book for class?

M _____ _____. It's starting to rain. I forgot my umbrella.

W My mom told me to put it in my bag, so _____ _____ _____.

M Good for you. Would you _____ _____ with me?

9 대화를 듣고, 남자가 새 바지를 사려고 하는 이유를 고르시오.

① 바지가 낡아서
② 축구복이 필요해서
③ 바지에 구멍이 나서
④ 바지의 얼룩이 지워지지 않아서

M Mom, can I have some money for a new pair of pants for school?

W Your pants are fine. _____ _____ _____ yesterday.

M Umm... I played soccer in them today. _____ _____ _____ _____ in them now. _____ _____ _____.

W Oh, no! There is a hole in your pants! Those pants are not cheap.

M I'm sorry, Mom.

10 대화를 듣고, 남자가 잘못 누른 전화번호의 개수를 고르시오.

① 1개
② 2개
③ 3개
④ 4개

[Telephone rings.]

M Hello. May I _____ _____ Mark?

W I'm sorry. There is no one here _____ _____ _____.

M Is this 936-2201?

W No, it's not. _____ _____ - _____.

M Then I have the wrong number. I'm sorry.

W That's OK.

11 다음을 듣고, 표의 내용과 일치하지 <u>않는</u> 것을 고르시오.

Name	Number of brothers	Number of sisters
Jinho	0	0
Sanghyun	1	0
Mihyun	1	2

① ② ③ ④

M ① Jinho is _____ _____ _____.

② Both Jinho and Sanghyun do not have a sister.

③ Sanghyun has _____ _____ _____ _____ Mihyun has.

④ Sanghyun _____ _____ _____ than Mihyun.

12 다음을 듣고, 두 사람의 대화가 <u>어색한</u> 것을 고르시오.

① ② ③ ④

① **W** What time are we meeting?

M It's 2:30 now. We are late.

② **W** How about _____ _____ _____ at the park after school?

M Sounds good. What about going with Peter?

③ **W** How do I _____ _____ _____ _____ ?

M Go straight and turn left at the corner.

④ **W** What about going to a concert together tomorrow?

M That's _____ _____ _____ .

13 대화를 듣고, 남자가 지불해야 될 금액을 고르시오.

① $120
② $140
③ $160
④ $200

M I'd like to _____ _____ _____ .

W The gold one or _____ _____ _____ ?

M The gold one. How much is it?

W $200. But...

M Wow, it's too expensive.

W But _____ _____ _____ today, sir. Our jewelry department is having a special sale.

M Great. I'll buy it then.

14 대화를 듣고, 대화가 이루어지는 장소를 고르시오.

① dentist's
② pharmacy
③ candy store
④ emergency room

M Hello, what is the problem, Mrs. Bloom?

W _____ _____ _____ _____ is broken. It's too painful.

M It's broken. How did it happen?

W I ate some hard candy. _____ _____ _____ hard candy.

M The candy _____ _____ _____ .

W I think so.

M _____ _____ some medicine for you.

15 대화를 듣고, 무엇에 관한 내용인지 고르시오.

① 분실물 신고하기
② 선물 품목 정하기
③ 생일 파티 장소 정하기
④ 옷에 어울리는 시계 고르기

M Dad doesn't need _____ _____.
W Yes, he does. Most of his clothes are _____ _____.
M No, he needs a watch. He lost his watch the other day.
W Really? I didn't know. OK. Let's get him a new watch _____ _____ _____.
M Yes, _____ _____ _____. Where is the shop?

16 다음을 듣고, 주어진 상황에서 할 수 있는 말로 가장 적절한 것을 고르시오.

① It's nice to meet you.
② I want to meet you.
③ Please introduce me.
④ What do you think about me?

M Your friend invites you to his house. His mother _____ _____ _____. You are meeting her _____ _____ _____ _____. Your friend introduces you. What would you _____ _____ _____ after your friend introduces you?

17 다음을 듣고, 그림의 상황에 가장 알맞은 대화를 고르시오.

① ② ③ ④

① **W** _____ _____ _____ _____ in the play.
   M Thank you. Did you really like it?
② **W** It's so exciting to go camping. _____ _____ _____?
   M I guess so. Did you find the way by a computer?
③ **W** Let's watch a DVD on your computer.
   M Great idea! How about an action movie?
④ **W** Martin, would you _____ _____ _____ _____ at my computer?
   M Is something wrong? Let me just check it.

18 대화를 듣고, 여자의 심경으로 가장 알맞은 것을 고르시오.

① annoyed
② excited
③ scared
④ brave

M You kicked the ball. You go and get it.
W It's in Mr. Jones' _____ _____.
M So go and get it.
W I can't. _____ _____ _____ _____ his dog.
M Really? It's only a small dog.
W But _____ _____ _____. It might bite me.

19 대화를 듣고, 남자의 마지막 말에 이어질 여자의 응답으로 가장 적절한 것을 고르시오.

① She is doing well.
② She is right over there.
③ She needs a new sweater.
④ My older sister is 18 years old.

M It was _____ _____ _____ _____, Pauline.
W Yes, it was nice to talk to you, too.
M _____ _____ _____ _____ now?
W No, I have to meet my sister. We're going to do some shopping together.
M Oh, how is _____ _____ _____?
W _____

20 대화를 듣고, 남자의 마지막 말에 이어질 여자의 응답으로 가장 적절한 것을 고르시오.

① Cook it medium-rare, please.
② Onion soup or vegetable soup.
③ Onion soup is my favorite.
④ Meat sauce spaghetti.

W And what would you like to have, sir?
M _____ _____ _____. Either the spaghetti or the steak. What would you recommend?
W The steak is very delicious, sir. It comes with vegetables, potatoes and soup.
M OK. I'll have the steak. _____ _____, _____.
W OK. _____ _____ _____ _____ would you like?
M What kind can I have?
W _____

1 다음을 듣고, 그림을 가장 적절하게 묘사한 것을 고르시오.

① ② ③ ④

2 다음을 듣고, 남자가 동물원에 가기 싫어하는 이유를 고르시오.

① 동물들을 별로 안 좋아해서
② 동물원이 너무 좁고 사람들로 붐벼서
③ 우리에 갇혀 있는 동물들이 불쌍해서
④ 야생동물들이 우리를 뚫고 나올까 무서워서

3 대화를 듣고, 남자가 가려고 하는 장소로 알맞은 것을 고르시오.

① 운동장 ② 헬스클럽
③ 구두 가게 ④ 신발 가게

4 대화를 듣고, 남자가 어제 한 일을 고르시오.

① 카드게임을 했다.
② 피자와 치킨을 먹었다.
③ 엄마의 병간호를 했다.
④ 엄마의 생신파티를 했다.

5 다음을 듣고, 무엇에 관한 내용인지 고르시오.

① 제일 좋아하는 과목 순위
② 오늘의 수업 시간표
③ 성적이 높은 과목 순위
④ 과목별 시험 일정표

6 다음을 듣고, 여자의 장래 희망으로 알맞은 것을 고르시오.

① teacher ② fashion model
③ fashion designer ④ fashion analyst

7 다음을 듣고, 두 사람의 대화가 <u>어색한</u> 것을 고르시오.

① ② ③ ④

8 다음을 듣고, 전화를 건 사람의 목적으로 알맞은 것을 고르시오.

① 영화 표를 예매하려고
② 직원과 직접 통화하려고
③ 영화의 상영 시간을 알아보려고
④ 상영 중인 영화 제목을 알아보려고

9 다음을 듣고, 남자에게 조언해줄 수 있는 속담으로 알맞은 것을 고르시오.

① Seeing is believing.
② Walls have ears.
③ There is no smoke without fire.
④ No news is good news.

10 다음을 듣고, 여자가 자기 엄마한테 말하지 <u>않을</u> 것을 고르시오.

① 돈가스를 먹은 것
② 친구네 집에서 저녁을 먹은 것
③ 친구 엄마가 요리를 잘 못한다는 것
④ 친구 엄마의 돈가스가 더 맛있다는 것

11 다음을 듣고, 무엇에 관한 설명인지 고르시오.

① ②

③ ④

12 대화를 듣고, 여자에게 공부하는 데에 도움이 되는
것을 고르시오.

① pop song
② classical music
③ water and snacks
④ concentration device

13 다음을 듣고, 주어진 상황에서 할 수 있는 말로 알맞
은 것을 고르시오.

① It's my pleasure.
② We'll have a good time.
③ I couldn't agree more.
④ Thank you very much.

14 다음을 듣고, 남자가 지난 일요일에 한 일을 순서대
로 나열한 것을 고르시오.

(A)  　　　　(B)

(C)

① (A)-(B)-(C)　　　　② (B)-(C)-(A)
③ (C)-(B)-(A)　　　　④ (C)-(A)-(B)

15 대화를 듣고, 남자가 지불할 총 금액을 고르시오.

① $30　　　　② $33
③ $34.5　　　　④ $35.5

16 대화를 듣고, 여자가 캐나다에 가는 목적을 고르시
오.

① 영어를 배우러　　　　② 친척을 만나러
③ 배낭 여행하러　　　　④ 친구를 만나러

17 대화를 듣고, 여자가 가고 싶어하는 장소를 고르시
오.

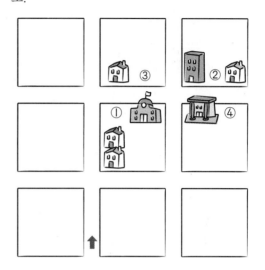

18 대화를 듣고, 여자의 기분으로 알맞은 것을 고르시
오.

① 깜짝 놀란
② 자랑스러운
③ 만족스러운
④ 무관심한

[19-20] 대화를 듣고, 여자의 마지막 말에 이어질 남자
의 응답으로 가장 적절한 것을 고르시오.

19

① I agree. The red one is better.
② Yes, it doesn't matter.
③ No problem. I'll buy it.
④ Yes, white is my favorite.

20

① Let's hurry and order.
② Don't worry. It's my treat.
③ You lost your wallet?
④ Thank you for paying for me.

1 다음을 듣고, 그림을 가장 적절하게 묘사한 것을 고르시오.

① ② ③ ④

W ① _____ _____ _____ _____ his big dog in the garden.

② A man is playing with his big dog in the garden.

③ A dog is barking _____ _____ _____.

④ A seeing-eye dog _____ _____ _____ _____.

2 다음을 듣고, 남자가 동물원에 가기 싫어하는 이유를 고르시오.

① 동물들을 별로 안 좋아해서
② 동물원이 너무 좁고 사람들로 붐벼서
③ 우리에 갇혀 있는 동물들이 불쌍해서
④ 야생동물들이 우리를 뚫고 나올까 무서워서

M I don't like to go to the zoo. I don't think animals should be _____ _____ _____. Wild animals like lions and tigers _____ _____ _____. They need _____ _____ _____ _____. When I think about the lions and tigers in the zoo, I feel sad. The animals can't be happy.

3 대화를 듣고, 남자가 가려고 하는 장소로 알맞은 것을 고르시오.

① 운동장
② 헬스클럽
③ 구두 가게
④ 신발 가게

M I want to buy _____ _____ _____.

W Really? I was shopping yesterday. The shoe store on Second Street has a big sale _____ _____ _____.

M Oh, _____ _____?

W Yes, it has lots of running shoes on sale.

M I'll go and buy some. Would you come with me?

4 대화를 듣고, 남자가 어제 한 일을 고르시오.

① 카드게임을 했다.
② 피자와 치킨을 먹었다.
③ 엄마의 병간호를 했다.
④ 엄마의 생신파티를 했다.

M What did everyone do at the birthday party yesterday?

W We ate pizza and chicken. And we _____ _____ _____ and other party games.

M Was it a lot of fun?

W Yes. _____ _____ _____ _____?

M My mom is very sick. I had to _____ _____ _____ _____ yesterday.

W Oh, that's too bad. I hope she feels better soon.

5 다음을 듣고, 무엇에 관한 내용인지 고르시오.

① 제일 좋아하는 과목 순위
② 오늘의 수업 시간표
③ 성적이 높은 과목 순위
④ 과목별 시험 일정표

W Today is Thursday. So let's see, we have English first. Then we have _____ _____. And right before lunch we have Korean history. Then after lunch we have _____ _____. My favorite subject is Korean literature. And I like the teacher very much. _____ _____ _____ _____ of the day are science and physical education.

6 다음을 듣고, 여자의 장래 희망으로 알맞은 것을 고르시오.

① teacher
② fashion model
③ fashion designer
④ fashion analyst

W Clothes are very important. We must look good _____ _____ _____. I love thinking about clothes. I wear a uniform to school, but on the weekend I wear something I like. It makes me happy when _____ _____ _____. In the future I want to make beautiful dresses with _____ _____ _____ _____.

7 다음을 듣고, 두 사람의 대화가 <u>어색한</u> 것을 고르시오.

①   ②   ③   ④

① **M** I like to watch baseball games. How about you?
  W I don't like to watch baseball. It's too slow.
② **M** My cell phone is broken. _____ _____ _____.
  W Oh, that's too bad. You should buy a new one.
③ **M** _____ _____ do you like to watch on TV?
  W Basketball. It's _____ _____ _____.
④ **M** I lost my school bag today in the subway.
  W You must be _____ _____ _____.

8 다음을 듣고, 전화를 건 사람의 목적으로 알맞은 것을 고르시오.

① 영화 표를 예매하려고
② 직원과 직접 통화하려고
③ 영화의 상영 시간을 알아보려고
④ 상영 중인 영화 제목을 알아보려고

W Hello, welcome to Megabox Movie Theater. Listen and _____ _____ _____ _____. Press one to make a reservation for a movie. Press two to find out the names of _____ _____ _____ right now. Press three to talk to someone. [pressing sound] In theater one, _____ _____ _____ *Indiana Johnson* is playing. In theater two, the romantic comedy *Sweetest Love* is playing. And in theater three, the horror film *Dracula* is playing.

9 다음을 듣고, 남자에게 조언해줄 수 있는 속담으로 알맞은 것을 고르시오.

① Seeing is believing.
② Walls have ears.
③ There is no smoke without fire.
④ No news is good news.

M One of my friends, Bill told me he was angry at another friend, Mike. Bill said bad things about Mike. Someone heard Bill and told Mike. Bill _____ _____ _____ _____ about others. And he must remember a famous English saying about _____ _____ _____ _____. It means other people are always listening.

10 다음을 듣고, 여자가 자기 엄마한테 말하지 않을 것을 고르시오.

① 돈가스를 먹은 것
② 친구네 집에서 저녁을 먹은 것
③ 친구 엄마가 요리를 잘 못한다는 것
④ 친구 엄마의 돈가스가 더 맛있다는 것

W Last night my friend's mother invited me to stay for dinner. We ate deep-fried _____ _____. The meat was delicious. My friend's mother cooked it very well. _____ _____ _____ _____ than my mother. But I will _____ _____ _____ to my mother.

11 다음을 듣고, 무엇에 관한 설명인지 고르시오.

① ②
③ ④

M I am _____ _____ that can fly. My body is round and I have a _____ _____ _____ _____ of my round body. I am _____ _____ _____ _____. I am harmless and do not hurt humans. What am I?

12 대화를 듣고, 여자에게 공부하는 데에 도움이 되는 것을 고르시오.

① pop song
② classical music
③ water and snacks
④ concentration device

M Doesn't that _____ _____ _____ _____ well?

W No, it helps me.

M I need water and snacks to help me study well. Music would just make me _____ _____ _____ _____. I couldn't study.

W Well, I don't listen to pop songs. I listen to classical music. So it _____ _____ _____.

M It wouldn't work for me. I like it when it's really quiet.

W Well, everyone is different.

13 다음을 듣고, 주어진 상황에서 할 수 있는 말로 알맞은 것을 고르시오.

① It's my pleasure.
② We'll have a good time.
③ I couldn't agree more.
④ Thank you very much.

W A friend asks where you are going. You say you are going to a shop downtown. The friend wants to _____ _____. You ask her if she wants a ride. You _____ _____ _____ _____. As she gets off the car, _____ _____ _____. In this situation, how _____ _____ _____ to your friend?

14 다음을 듣고, 남자가 지난 일요일에 한 일을 순서대로 나열한 것을 고르시오.

(A)   (B)

(C)

① (A)–(B)–(C)   ② (B)–(C)–(A)
③ (C)–(B)–(A)   ④ (C)–(A)–(B)

M My family _____ _____ _____ _____ last Sunday. At the park we played badminton. Then we _____ _____ _____ _____ _____. After boating, we were hungry so we ate gimbap. After lunch, we rested _____ _____ _____. It was very hot, so we didn't play anymore. We slept for half an hour.

15 대화를 듣고, 남자가 지불할 총 금액을 고르시오.

① $30
② $33
③ $34.5
④ $35.5

M How is the food here?

W Good. _____ _____ _____. How much is the bill?

M Let me see. It's $30.

W Do you want me to _____ _____ _____?

M No, Theresa, I will _____ _____ _____ this time. Is 10% enough?

W Yes, it is. Thanks for dinner.

16 대화를 듣고, 여자가 캐나다에 가는 목적을 고르시오.

① 영어를 배우러
② 친척을 만나러
③ 배낭 여행하러
④ 친구를 만나러

W I will leave for Canada next week. I'm so excited.

M Are you going to Canada _____ _____ _____?

W I told you I'm _____ _____ _____ and I'd like to go to a famous museum, if I have a chance.

M That's right. I forgot. So how long will you be there?

W _____ _____ _____.

M Don't you have some friends in Canada?

W You mean John? Actually he is from the United States.

17 대화를 듣고, 여자가 가고 싶어하는 장소를 고르시오.

W _____ _____. Can you tell me where _____ _____ _____ _____?

M Go straight for two blocks _____ _____ _____. Walk for a few minutes. It's across the street from City Hall.

W Go straight for two blocks and turn right. _____ _____ _____ City Hall.

M No, _____ _____ _____ _____ from City Hall.

W OK. Across the street from City Hall. I got it.

18 대화를 듣고, 여자의 기분으로 알맞은 것을 고르시오.

① 깜짝 놀란
② 자랑스러운
③ 만족스러운
④ 무관심한

M Today my teacher told us _____ _____ _____ _____. How were your test scores?

W _____ _____ _____.

M Not too bad! What do you mean?

W I got _____ _____ _____ I would get.

M _____ _____ _____.

W I am satisfied. I wanted to do better, but the scores I got are OK.

19 대화를 듣고, 여자의 마지막 말에 이어질 남자의 응답으로 가장 적절한 것을 고르시오.

① I agree. The red one is better.
② Yes, it doesn't matter.
③ No problem. I'll buy it.
④ Yes, white is my favorite.

W Paul, which shirt do you like better?

M _____ _____ _____ the red one or the blue one?

W Yes, I think _____ _____ _____ in blue.

M Really?

W Yes, I do.

M Either one is fine, Mom. I don't _____ _____ _____ _____.

W Really?

M _____

20 대화를 듣고, 여자의 마지막 말에 이어질 남자의 응답으로 가장 적절한 것을 고르시오.

① Let's hurry and order.
② Don't worry. It's my treat.
③ You lost your wallet?
④ Thank you for paying for me.

M It's warm and sunny. Don't you think this is a good park?

W Yes, it is. I'm happy to take a walk with you.

M Do you want to go and get _____ _____ _____?

W Yes, _____ _____ _____.

M What do you want to have? Hamburgers or sandwiches?

W _____ _____ _____ some gimbap.

M OK. Sounds like a good idea.

W Oh, no. I forgot I don't have any money _____ _____ _____.

M _____

A Write down the definition of each word or phrase.

1	dish		11	stranger
2	weigh		12	stuff
3	fitness center		13	chores
4	violence		14	literature
5	educational		15	analyst
6	poison		16	insect
7	jewelry		17	concentrate
8	bite		18	device
9	frightened (of~)		19	relatives
10	bark		20	satisfied

B Match each word with the right definition.

1	spot		a	계단
2	bill		b	혀, 말, 언어
3	care about		c	공유하다, 함께 쓰다
4	fall down		d	부러진, 깨진, 고장 난
5	share		e	처방하다
6	tongue		f	며칠 전에, 요전날
7	prescribe		g	연기하다, 연주하다
8	broken		h	눈 먼, 맹인의
9	leave for		i	조화시키다, 어울리다
10	match		j	넘어지다, 구르다
11	stair		k	점, 지점, 장소
12	perform		l	해롭지 않은, 무해한
13	the other day		m	계산서, 청구서
14	blind		n	~로 떠나다
15	harmless		o	~을 신경 쓰다

C Choose the best answer for the blank.

1 I didn't go to the fitness center. Nor _____ sports.

 a. I played b. did I play c. I didn't play

2 Would you mind _____ a look at my computer?

 a. have b. to have c. having

3 She is now _____ in Seoul or in Tokyo.

 a. either b. neither c. both

4 That music stops me _____ studying well.

 a. off b. by c. from

5 I'd like to _____ a reservation for a round-trip ticket, Seoul to New York.

 a. put b. make c. take

6 Please do not reply _____ this email.

 a. to b. by c. for

D Complete the short dialogues.

1 A: What's wrong with you?

 B: My car is broken. Can you give me a _____ to the airport?

2 A: May I speak with Tom?

 B: I'm sorry. You must have the _____ number. There is no one here by that name.

3 A: I lost a lot of weight just by walking to work instead of taking a bus.

 B: Small changes can make a big _____.

4 A: Which shirt do you like better?

 B: It doesn't _____. Either one is fine.

5 A: How about seeing a movie tonight?

 B: OK. I'll find _____ the names of the movies playing right now first.

1 다음을 듣고, 현장학습에 가지 <u>않는</u> 학생들이 하는 일을 고르시오.

① 집에서 과제를 한다.
② 학교에서 청소를 한다.
③ 학교 도서관에서 공부한다.
④ 도서관에서 도서를 정리한다.

2 대화를 듣고, 남자의 직업으로 알맞은 것을 고르시오.

① boss
② deliveryperson
③ computer repairperson
④ computer salesperson

3 다음을 듣고, 주어진 상황에서 할 수 있는 말로 알맞은 것을 고르시오.

① No thanks. I'm full.
② It's OK. My glass is full.
③ Yes. That would be nice.
④ You're a really good cook.

4 대화를 듣고, 남자가 우체국에 가는 이유를 고르시오.

① 우표를 사러   ② 소포를 보내러
③ 편지 부치러   ④ 소포를 받으러

5 대화를 듣고, 남자가 찾는 곳을 고르시오.

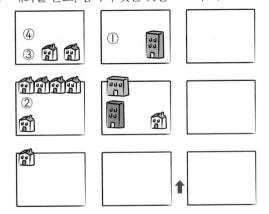

6 대화를 듣고, 여자가 가야 할 곳이 <u>아닌</u> 것을 고르시오.

① 사진관
② 미용실
③ 세탁소
④ 슈퍼마켓

7 다음을 듣고, 남자가 전화를 한 목적을 고르시오.

① 진료 예약
② 약속 취소
③ 검사 결과 통보
④ 약속 장소 변경

8 대화를 듣고, 여자가 남자에게 권하는 것을 고르시오.

① 과자 줄이기
② 체중 감량하기
③ 식사 거르지 않기
④ 건강에 좋은 음식 먹기

9 대화를 듣고, 여자가 지난 주말에 한 일을 고르시오.

① 영화 보기
② 음식 만들기
③ 시험 공부하기
④ 집에서 쉬기

10 다음을 듣고, 두 사람의 대화가 <u>어색한</u> 것을 고르시오.

①   ②   ③   ④

11 대화를 듣고, 여자가 한 일을 순서대로 바르게 나열한 것을 고르시오.

(A)

(B)

(C)

① (A)-(B)-(C)
② (A)-(C)-(B)
③ (B)-(A)-(C)
④ (C)-(B)-(A)

12 대화를 듣고, 남자가 지불하게 될 금액을 고르시오.
① $8   ② $10
③ $14   ④ $20

13 대화를 듣고, 남자의 심정으로 알맞은 것을 고르시오.
① 걱정스러운
② 귀찮은
③ 짜증나는
④ 지루한

14 다음을 듣고, 내용과 일치하지 <u>않는</u> 것을 고르시오.
① 액션 영화에 관한 광고이다.
② 영화에서 James Bond는 스파이이다.
③ 이 영화는 다음 주 금요일에 개봉한다.
④ 이 영화의 시리즈는 10번째까지 개봉되었다.

15 대화를 듣고, 두 사람이 무엇에 관해 이야기하고 있는지를 고르시오.
① 저녁 식사 메뉴
② 감기에 좋은 음식
③ 엄마가 제일 잘하는 요리
④ 닭고기 수프 조리법

16 다음을 듣고, 그림의 상황에 가장 알맞은 대화를 고르시오.

①   ②   ③   ④

17 대화를 듣고, 두 사람의 관계로 알맞은 것을 고르시오.
① 팬 – 배우
② 배우 – 극장 직원
③ 관객 – 취재 기자
④ 영화평론가 – 감독

18 대화를 듣고, 내용과 일치하지 <u>않는</u> 것을 고르시오.
① 남자는 외동아들이다.
② 남자는 여행이 재미없었다.
③ 남자는 가끔 외로움을 느낀다.
④ 남자는 혼자 바닷가에 놀러 갔다.

[19-20] 대화를 듣고, 남자의 마지막 말에 이어질 여자의 응답으로 가장 적절한 것을 고르시오.

19
① Well done! Good for you.
② That's too bad.
③ I'll help you finish it now.
④ Next time don't give up!

20
① Don't worry, I'll help you.
② Come right this way, please.
③ Don't mention it at all.
④ Will you help me with this problem?

1 다음을 듣고, 현장학습에 가지 <u>않는</u> 학생들이 하는 일을 고르시오.

① 집에서 과제를 한다.
② 학교에서 청소를 한다.
③ 학교 도서관에서 공부한다.
④ 도서관에서 도서를 정리한다.

M Can I _____ _____ _____, please? Only two students will not be going on tomorrow's field trip. They must still come to school. They will study in the library. _____ _____ _____ _____ _____. Students going on the field trip must be at school by 9 a.m. Students not going _____ _____ _____ _____ must go to the library at 8:30.

2 대화를 듣고, 남자의 직업으로 알맞은 것을 고르시오.

① boss
② deliveryperson
③ computer repairperson
④ computer salesperson

W My boss's computer has a problem.
M Where is his computer?
W In his office. Follow me, please. *[pause]* He said it might _____ _____ _____.
M Well, I'll find the problem _____ _____ _____.
W How long will it take?
M I need to know the problem _____ _____ _____ _____. If it's a hardware problem, I will have to take the computer _____ _____ _____ _____.

3 다음을 듣고, 주어진 상황에서 할 수 있는 말로 알맞은 것을 고르시오.

① No thanks. I'm full.
② It's OK. My glass is full.
③ Yes. That would be nice.
④ You're a really good cook.

W It is dinner time. Mark is eating dinner with his family. He finishes _____ _____ _____. His mother thinks he is still hungry. His mother asks him if he wants _____ _____ _____. But he doesn't want any more rice. _____ _____ _____ _____. In this situation, what would Mark say to his mother?

4 대화를 듣고, 남자가 우체국에 가는 이유를 고르시오.

① 우표를 사러
② 소포를 보내러
③ 편지를 부치러
④ 소포를 받으러

M I have to go to the post office.

W _____ _____ _____ _____ .

M I don't need stamps. We _____ _____ _____ from the post office.

W What did they say?

M _____ _____ _____ _____ to be picked up.

W Oh, it must be a present from your mom. Your birthday is next week.

---

5 대화를 듣고, 남자가 찾는 곳을 고르시오.

M Excuse me, can you tell me where the library is?

W Sure. Go straight for two blocks and turn left. And then walk for two more blocks and turn right. The library will be _____ _____ _____ in the middle of the block.

M Walk two blocks and turn left. Then _____ _____ _____ and turn right.

W That's right. It's on your right _____ _____ _____ _____ the block.

M Thank you.

---

6 대화를 듣고, 여자가 가야 할 곳이 <u>아닌</u> 것을 고르시오.

① 사진관
② 미용실
③ 세탁소
④ 슈퍼마켓

M Where are you going, Mom?

W I have _____ _____ _____ _____ to do. I have to go to the dry cleaner's and the bakery on 4th Avenue.

M Oh, can you buy a piece of cake for me?

W Sure. I also have to go to the supermarket _____ _____ _____ _____ .

M OK. See you _____ _____ _____ _____ .

7 다음을 듣고, 남자가 전화를 한 목적을 고르시오.

① 진료 예약
② 약속 취소
③ 검사 결과 통보
④ 약속 장소 변경

[Beep, Beep]

M This is Doctor Doolittle's Office. I'm sorry but the doctor has to _____ _____ _____ tomorrow. He must go to a doctor's meeting downtown. Please _____ _____ _____ as soon as possible _____ _____ _____ a new time. I am sorry to have to cancel the appointment.

8 대화를 듣고, 여자가 남자에게 권하는 것을 고르시오.

① 과자 줄이기
② 체중 감량하기
③ 식사 거르지 않기
④ 건강에 좋은 음식 먹기

M I'm so busy that it's hard to do. I don't have time _____ _____ _____.

W I always _____ _____ _____ in my bags.

M What kind of snacks?

W Fresh fruit like bananas and apples, and sometimes rice cakes.

M I guess I shouldn't have hamburgers and fries for lunch.

W You'll feel better _____ _____ _____ _____.

M I hope so. I'm tired all the time these days.

9 대화를 듣고, 여자가 지난 주말에 한 일을 고르시오.

① 영화 보기
② 음식 만들기
③ 시험 공부하기
④ 집에서 쉬기

M So what movie did you see last weekend?

W I didn't see a movie.

M Really? You always go to a movie with your friends on the weekend.

W _____ _____ _____. Exams are next week. I stayed home and studied.

M That's what I should have done, too. But _____ _____ _____ _____ at home and made some cookies with my mom.

W Well, we _____ _____ _____ _____ for next week.

10 다음을 듣고, 두 사람의 대화가 <u>어색한</u> 것을 고르시오.

① ② ③ ④

① **M** Are you interested _____ _____?

　 W Yes, I'm interested in the sun and stars.

② **M** What a nice sweater! _____ _____ _____.

　 W I'm glad you like it.

③ **M** You look sick. What's the matter?

　 W I have had a toothache since last night.

④ **M** How about going to _____ _____ _____ this weekend?

　 W That's a good idea. You should _____ _____ _____.

11 대화를 듣고, 여자가 한 일을 순서대로 바르게 나열한 것을 고르시오.

(A)　　　　(B)

(C)

① (A)-(B)-(C)
② (A)-(C)-(B)
③ (B)-(A)-(C)
④ (C)-(B)-(A)

M Were you busy this morning?

W Yes, I drove Sarah to school.

M Did you come home _____ _____?

W No, I bought some food _____ _____ _____.

M _____ _____ _____ the house?

W Yes, I cleaned the house.

M So now you're _____ _____ _____.

W Yes, I am resting now and drinking coffee.

12 대화를 듣고, 남자가 지불하게 될 금액을 고르시오.

① $8
② $10
③ $14
④ $20

W Good evening, sir. I'm selling cookies and chocolates.

M How much _____ _____ _____?

W Cookies are $4 a box and the chocolates are $10 a box.

M That's expensive.

W Sir, the money goes to _____ _____ _____ without parents.

M Hmm. OK. I'll _____ _____ _____ of cookies.

13 대화를 듣고, 남자의 심정으로 알맞은 것을 고르시오.

① 걱정스러운
② 귀찮은
③ 짜증나는
④ 지루한

M _____ _____ _____ so much!

W But I am trying to find something to watch.

M You can't find it if you keep changing the channel.

W _____ _____ _____ _____ . What do you want to watch on TV?

M I don't care what we watch. _____ _____ _____ _____ one station. Don't change channels so much.

14 다음을 듣고, 내용과 일치하지 <u>않는</u> 것을 고르시오.

① 액션 영화에 관한 광고이다.
② 영화에서 James Bond는 스파이이다.
③ 이 영화는 다음 주 금요일에 개봉한다.
④ 이 영화의 시리즈는 10번째까지 이미 개봉되었다.

W It's the greatest action movie ever! James Bond is the world's _____ _____ ! He saves the world from the evil Dr. No! The opening night _____ _____ _____ _____ in the James Bond series is next Friday. Check theaters for times and dates. And check out the James Bond website. www.jamesbond.com.

15 대화를 듣고, 두 사람이 무엇에 관해 이야기하고 있는지를 고르시오.

① 저녁 식사 메뉴
② 감기에 좋은 음식
③ 엄마가 제일 잘하는 요리
④ 닭고기 수프 조리법

M You should drink hot water _____ _____ _____ _____ in it.

W Will it _____ _____ _____ ?

M Yes, it'll help you.

W When I was a child, my mom _____ _____ _____ _____ .

M That's right. But I can't make you chicken soup now. I'll bring you a glass of honey and water instead. _____ _____ _____ .

16 다음을 듣고, 그림의 상황에 가장 알맞은 대화를 고르시오.

① ② ③ ④

① **M** Is he reading science books?

W No, he isn't. He is _____ _____ _____ _____ an elephant now.

② **M** Can you play the piano for the elephants?

W _____ _____ _____ _____ . It's too late at night.

③ **M** I really enjoyed your class. Thank you very much.

W I was happy to be with you, too.

④ **M** You know what? _____ _____ _____ .

W Oh, really? That's interesting. I didn't know that.

17 대화를 듣고, 두 사람의 관계로 알맞은 것을 고르시오.

① 팬 – 배우
② 배우 – 극장 직원
③ 관객 – 취재 기자
④ 영화평론가 – 감독

M I'm so happy to see you _____ _____. I really love all your movies.

W Thank you. Do you have a favorite _____ _____ _____?

M *Seven Days in Seattle*. It was a great love story.

W I think it is a very good movie, too.

M _____ _____ _____ this piece of paper for me?

W Yes, I can.

18 대화를 듣고, 내용과 일치하지 <u>않는</u> 것을 고르시오.

① 남자는 외동아들이다.
② 남자는 여행이 재미없었다.
③ 남자는 가끔 외로움을 느낀다.
④ 남자는 혼자 바닷가에 놀러 갔다.

M My family took a trip to the beach on Saturday.

W Sounds like fun.

M Not really. Mom and Dad talked _____ _____ _____. In the car. At the beach. _____ _____ _____ _____.

W You need a brother or a sister.

M Yeah. That would be nice. _____ _____ _____ all the time, but sometimes it would be nice to have someone to play with.

19 대화를 듣고, 남자의 마지막 말에 이어질 여자의 응답으로 가장 적절한 것을 고르시오.

① Well done! Good for you.
② That's too bad.
③ I'll help you finish it now.
④ Next time don't give up!

W Wow! You did make this model by yourself.

M Yes, it's a model of my favorite car.

W _____ _____ _____ _____.

M Yes, over 100. Yesterday _____ _____ _____ _____. I wanted to stop.

W You thought it was too hard.

M Yes, but I didn't give up. And I finished it today.

W _____

20 대화를 듣고, 남자의 마지막 말에 이어질 여자의 응답으로 가장 적절한 것을 고르시오.

① Don't worry, I'll help you.
② Come right this way, please.
③ Don't mention it at all.
④ Will you help me with this problem?

W What's wrong? _____ _____ _____.

M Yes, I hate math.

W Do you _____ _____ _____ some homework?

M Yes, it's this math problem.

W Is it difficult for you? How about other questions?

M I solved all of them _____ _____ _____ _____. I can't solve only one. I keep getting the wrong answer.

W _____

1 다음을 듣고, 무엇에 관한 설명인지 고르시오.

①  ②

③  ④

2 다음을 듣고, 아들에 대해 <u>틀린</u> 것을 고르시오.

① 작년에 공부를 열심히 하지 않았다.
② 작년의 실수를 되풀이하고 있다.
③ 작년에 수학을 잘 못했다.
④ 올해는 열심히 공부한다.

3 대화를 듣고, 내용과 일치하지 <u>않는</u> 것을 고르시오.

① 여자는 Sue를 두 달 전에 봤다.
② Sue는 지금 벤치에 앉아 있다.
③ 남자는 Sue를 세 달 만에 봤다.
④ 그들은 Sue와 공원에서 만나기로 했다.

4 대화를 듣고, 여자가 의사가 되려는 이유로 알맞은 것을 고르시오.

① 이 도시에서 병원을 열고 싶어서
② 전국을 돌며 의료봉사를 하고 싶어서
③ 시골에서 가난한 사람들을 돕고 싶어서
④ 가난한 나라에서 아픈 사람들을 돕고 싶어서

5 대화를 듣고, 두 사람의 관계로 가장 알맞은 것을 고르시오.

① 엄마 – 아들
② 식당 직원 – 고객
③ 택시 운전사 – 손님
④ 태권도 선생님 – 학생

6 대화를 듣고, 여자가 전화를 건 목적으로 알맞은 것을 고르시오.

① 경찰을 부르려고
② 화재를 신고하려고
③ 호텔의 위치를 물어보려고
④ 불꽃놀이 장소를 물어보려고

7 대화를 듣고, 두 사람이 만든 눈사람의 모습을 고르시오.

①   ②

③   ④

8 대화를 듣고, 괴물에 대한 남자의 상상이 <u>아닌</u> 것을 고르시오.

① 팔이 여섯 개다.
② 침대 밑에 산다.
③ 아이들을 잡아먹는다.
④ 방을 살살 돌아다닌다.

9 대화를 듣고, 여자가 PC방에 온 이유로 알맞은 것을 고르시오.

① 친구를 만나러
② 컴퓨터 게임을 하러
③ 컴퓨터 숙제를 하러
④ 친구에게 이메일을 보내러

10 대화를 듣고, 남자가 다시 입어보려고 하는 셔츠의 사이즈를 고르시오.

① 95
② 100
③ 105
④ 110

11 다음을 듣고, 표의 내용과 일치하지 <u>않는</u> 것을 고르시오.

Name	Age	Weight
Mary	14	39kg
Sally	11	36kg
Tony	14	63kg

① ② ③ ④

12 다음을 듣고, 두 사람의 대화가 <u>어색한</u> 것을 고르시오.

① ② ③ ④

13 대화를 듣고, 남자가 여자에게 빌려주려고 하는 금액을 고르시오.

① $30
② $60
③ $90
④ $150

14 대화를 듣고, 무슨 상황에 관한 내용인지 고르시오.

① 호텔 시설 문의
② 호텔 입실 절차
③ 호텔 퇴실 절차
④ 호텔 위치 문의

15 다음을 듣고, 주어진 상황에서 할 수 있는 말로 가장 적절한 것을 고르시오.

① Go home and rest.
② It's time to get up.
③ Go and see a doctor.
④ I hope you feel better soon.

16 대화를 듣고, 여자가 오랫동안 손을 씻고 있는 이유를 고르시오.

① 손에 기름때가 묻어서
② 손에 페인트가 묻어서
③ 손에서 페인트 냄새가 나서
④ 손에 장갑이 눌러 붙어서

17 다음을 듣고, 그림의 상황에 가장 알맞은 대화를 고르시오.

① ② ③ ④

18 대화를 듣고, 여자의 심경으로 가장 알맞은 것을 고르시오.

① envious
② disappointed
③ surprised
④ worried

[19-20] 대화를 듣고, 여자의 마지막 말에 이어질 남자의 응답으로 가장 적절한 것을 고르시오.

19

① For four people.
② For four o'clock.
③ Yes, the 14th.
④ I need four tickets.

20

① My family will travel to America.
② School was very hard this year.
③ Are you good at swimming?
④ Summer is almost over.

1 다음을 듣고, 무엇에 관한 설명인지 고르시오.

① ② ③ ④

W This is a very large building. There can sometimes be over 60,000 or 70,000 people in this. The people sit down on seats which look down _____ _____ _____ _____. The playing field is sometimes _____ _____ _____ _____ and sometimes it is not. People usually go here to _____ _____ _____ _____ play a game, for example, soccer or baseball.

2 다음을 듣고, 아들에 대해 **틀린** 것을 고르시오.

① 작년에 공부를 열심히 하지 않았다.
② 작년의 실수를 되풀이하고 있다.
③ 작년에 수학을 잘 못했다.
④ 올해는 열심히 공부한다.

M Mrs. Hanson talks to her son a lot. She wants him to be a good son. But she knows he will make mistakes. Last year he didn't study hard and _____ _____ _____ _____. So this year he is studying hard. Mrs. Hanson is happy that her son _____ _____ _____ _____. It reminds her of _____ _____ _____ that experience is the best teacher.

3 대화를 듣고, 내용과 일치하지 <u>않는</u> 것을 고르시오.

① 여자는 Sue를 두 달 전에 봤다.
② Sue는 지금 벤치에 앉아 있다.
③ 남자는 Sue를 세 달 만에 봤다.
④ 그들은 Sue와 공원에서 만나기로 했다.

M How is Sue? Are you _____ _____ _____ _____ her?
W No, I don't know. The last time I saw her was two months ago.
M I saw her _____ _____ _____.
W I hope she is fine. I'll contact her this weekend.
M Look! There she is now. She is sitting _____ _____ _____ _____.
W Wow! It's true if you talk about someone, there they are!

4 대화를 듣고, 여자가 의사가 되려는 이유로 알맞은 것을 고르시오.

① 이 도시에서 병원을 열고 싶어서
② 전국을 돌며 의료봉사를 하고 싶어서
③ 시골에서 가난한 사람들을 돕고 싶어서
④ 가난한 나라에서 아픈 사람들을 돕고 싶어서

M You will be a good doctor.
W Thank you. It's hard work, but I like to work hard.
M Will you _____ _____ _____ in this city?
W No, I want to help sick people in poor countries.
M Really? There are many sick people in this city. Don't you want to _____ _____?
W No, this is what I want. I don't want to work _____ _____ _____ _____.

5 대화를 듣고, 두 사람의 관계로 가장 알맞은 것을 고르시오.

① 엄마 – 아들
② 식당 직원 – 고객
③ 택시 운전사 – 손님
④ 태권도 선생님 – 학생

W It's time to go to Taekwondo class. I'll drive you to your Taekwondo class.

M Thanks. Can you _____ _____ _____, too?

W No, I can't. I have to take your sister shopping.

M OK. _____ _____ _____.

W _____ _____ _____ after the class. Don't run too fast.

M Yes, I will. Oh, what time will we go out to have dinner?

W We have to be at the restaurant at 7 p.m.

6 대화를 듣고, 여자가 전화를 건 목적으로 알맞은 것을 고르시오.

① 경찰을 부르려고
② 화재를 신고하려고
③ 호텔의 위치를 물어보려고
④ 불꽃놀이 장소를 물어보려고

[Telephone rings.]

M Hello. District One Fire Department.

W There is _____ _____ _____ coming out of a building on Main Street.

M Smoke? Main Street? _____ _____?

W It's the Grand Hotel. I think _____ _____ _____.

M OK. Thank you. Fire trucks are on their way.

W There is a lot of traffic around the hotel.

M Oh, really? Then I'll _____ _____ _____ _____ right away.

7 대화를 듣고, 두 사람이 만든 눈사람의 모습을 고르시오.

① ② ③ ④

W We have made a snowman. What do you think?

M He seems to be _____ _____ and he has _____ _____ _____.

W Can I use your hat for our snowman?

M Sure. Here it is. _____ _____ _____ _____ for our snowman.

W OK. Let's make a second one. The second snowman will wear red glasses _____ _____ _____.

8 대화를 듣고, 괴물에 대한 남자의 상상이 아닌 것을 고르시오.

① 팔이 여섯 개다.
② 침대 밑에 산다.
③ 아이들을 잡아먹는다.
④ 방을 살살 돌아다닌다.

M When I was a young child, I thought a monster lived _____ _____ _____.

W Really?

M Yeah. I believed _____ _____ _____ _____ and three eyes.

W Yikes! _____!

M Many times I heard it eating food. I thought it ate children. So I walked around the room carefully.

W You seemed very quiet, but sometimes _____ _____ _____ _____.

9 대화를 듣고, 여자가 PC방에 온 이유로 알맞은 것을 고르시오.

① 친구를 만나러
② 컴퓨터 게임을 하러
③ 컴퓨터 숙제를 하러
④ 친구에게 이메일을 보내러

M Hi, Lisa.

W Hi, Paul.

M You don't like computer games. What are you doing here in the PC room?

W I'm here to meet Bill.

M He's playing games on a computer _____ _____ _____.

W Thanks. We are going to have a cola and talk about _____ _____ _____. And we have to send an e-mail about the project to the teacher.

10 대화를 듣고, 남자가 다시 입어보려고 하는 셔츠의 사이즈를 고르시오.

① 95
② 100
③ 105
④ 110

M I tried on this shirt. And it is too large.

W So you need _____ _____ _____. Is that size 105?

M No, it's not. It's size 100.

W OK. I'll _____ _____ _____ _____.

M I usually wear a size 100.

W That company makes clothes a little larger than other companies.

M Then I'll _____ _____ _____ _____ a smaller size.

11 다음을 듣고, 표의 내용과 일치하지 <u>않는</u>
것을 고르시오.

Name	Age	Weight
Mary	14	39kg
Sally	11	36kg
Tony	14	63kg

① ② ③ ④

W ① _____ _____ _____ _____ than Tony.

② Mary is as heavy as Sally.

③ Sally is _____ _____ _____ _____ Mary.

④ Tony is _____ _____ .

12 다음을 듣고, 두 사람의 대화가 <u>어색한</u> 것
을 고르시오.

① ② ③ ④

① **M** Your report is great. You did a great job!

W That's _____ _____ _____ _____ to say so.

② **M** Thank you for cooking lunch. It's delicious.

W _____ _____ you like it.

③ **M** Do I know you?

W I don't think so. I don't think _____ _____ _____

_____ .

④ **M** You are late for class again. Don't you have a watch?

W I want to buy _____ _____ .

13 대화를 듣고, 남자가 여자에게 빌려주려고
하는 금액을 고르시오.

① $30
② $60
③ $90
④ $150

M Do you like this dress? How much is the dress?

W It's $150, but I don't have _____ _____ _____ in my
wallet.

M Do you have _____ _____ _____ ?

W No. I don't like to use a credit card because I think credit cards
_____ _____ _____ .

M Then how much money do you have right now?

W All I have is $90.

M I'll _____ _____ _____ _____ of the money, if you
want.

14 대화를 듣고, 무슨 상황에 관한 내용인지 고르시오.

① 호텔 시설 문의
② 호텔 입실 절차
③ 호텔 퇴실 절차
④ 호텔 위치 문의

M I'd like to _____ _____, please.

W _____. Can I have your room key?

M Here it is.

W Let's see Room 4005, Mr. Smith.

M Yes, _____ _____ _____ _____ in a room with a double bed.

W Yes, here is your bill. The total is $350.

M Can I _____ _____ _____? *[pause]* Let's see, telephone, dinner... Hmm... Everything is fine.

W How will you be paying?

M Here is my credit card.

15 다음을 듣고, 주어진 상황에서 할 수 있는 말로 가장 적절한 것을 고르시오.

① Go home and rest.
② It's time to get up.
③ Go and see a doctor.
④ I hope you feel better soon.

M Your friend is sick. He has a terrible cold. He _____ _____ _____ yesterday. He got some medicine. And he took some medicine this morning. But he is _____ _____ _____ _____ in class. He should go home. What would you say to him?

16 대화를 듣고, 여자가 오랫동안 손을 씻고 있는 이유를 고르시오.

① 손에 기름때가 묻어서
② 손에 페인트가 묻어서
③ 손에서 페인트 냄새가 나서
④ 손에 장갑이 눌러 붙어서

M Why are you washing your hands for such a long time?

W I have just painted _____ _____ _____. Didn't you see it?

M I didn't notice that, but I can smell the paint now. Do you have _____ _____ _____ _____?

W Yes, and _____ _____ _____ _____ _____.

M OK. You _____ _____ _____ when you paint.

W I will next time.

17 다음을 듣고, 그림의 상황에 가장 알맞은 대화를 고르시오.

① ② ③ ④

① M Good evening, ma'am. How may I help you?

W Well, I'm looking for _____ _____ _____ _____.

② M Would you be interested in coming with me to a movie?

W Sure. Let's go see a _____ _____.

③ M Welcome to the center. How may I help you?

M Well, what are _____ _____ _____ _____ these things?

④ M Did something happen? Why are you late?

W I'm so sorry. I went to _____ _____ _____.

18 대화를 듣고, 여자의 심경으로 가장 알맞은 것을 고르시오.

① envious
② disappointed
③ surprised
④ worried

W I thought I did poorly on the test. It was difficult for me.

M But you got a good score. So the teacher praised you _____ _____ _____.

W Yes, but _____ _____ _____ _____.

M Believe it. You got one of _____ _____ _____ in the class.

W I'll keep working hard.

19 대화를 듣고, 여자의 마지막 말에 이어질 남자의 응답으로 가장 적절한 것을 고르시오.

① For four people.
② For four o'clock.
③ Yes, the 14th.
④ I need four tickets.

[Telephone rings.]

W Good afternoon. Skyview 56 restaurant. How may I help you?

M _____ _____ _____, I want to know the location of your restaurant.

W It's near Namsan Tower.

M Oh, I see. I have an important meeting. I'd like to _____ _____ _____.

W _____ _____, sir?

M Wednesday, the 14th of May.

W OK. _____ _____ _____ _____?

M _____

20 대화를 듣고, 여자의 마지막 말에 이어질 남자의 응답으로 가장 적절한 것을 고르시오.

① My family will travel to America.
② School was very hard this year.
③ Are you good at swimming?
④ Summer is almost over.

M Theresa, how are you?

W I'm fine. I haven't seen you for a long time.

M Yes, _____ _____ _____ _____ _____. Long time no see. Are you busy this summer?

W Yes, I guess so. I have many lessons. Piano, swimming and art. I don't have time to play _____ _____ _____.

M Oh, I see.

W What are you going to do _____ _____?

M _____

TEST

18

A Write down the definition of each word or phrase.

1	librarian	**11**	instead	
2	repair shop	**12**	give up	
3	notice	**13**	except	
4	parcel	**14**	contact	
5	errand	**15**	wealthy	
6	avenue	**16**	district	
7	rice cake	**17**	chilly	
8	palace	**18**	wallet	
9	alone	**19**	effort	
10	evil	**20**	location	

B Match each word with the right definition.

1	take a break	_____	**a**	가득 찬, 충만한, 배부른
2	first of all	_____	**b**	되도록 빨리, 가능한 한 빨리
3	score	_____	**c**	잠시 휴식을 취하다, 잠깐 쉬다
4	full	_____	**d**	~없이, ~이 없는
5	praise	_____	**e**	~을 내려다보다
6	as soon as possible	_____	**f**	예를 들면
7	for example	_____	**g**	경험
8	horrible	_____	**h**	소방서
9	without	_____	**i**	무서운, 오싹한
10	check out	_____	**j**	~을 입어 보다, 시험 삼아 해보다
11	experience	_____	**k**	계산을 치르고 호텔에서 나오다, 확인하다
12	try on	_____	**l**	한번 보다, 대충 훑어보다
13	fire department	_____	**m**	점수, 성적
14	look over	_____	**n**	칭찬하다
15	look down on	_____	**o**	우선, 무엇보다 먼저

C Choose the best answer for the blank.

1 Why don't you quit _____?

    a. to smoke   b. smoking   c. a smoker

2 You remind me _____ your mother.

    a. of   b. with   c. to

3 Are you keeping _____ with him?

    a. a touch   b. in touch   c. touching

4 The hotel is _____ fire.

    a. with   b. in   c. on

5 We should _____ up a time to talk.

    a. make   b. build   c. set

6 Can I go home now? I'm _____ sick to study in class.

    a. too   b. so   c. very

D Complete the short dialogues.

1 A: Are you going to travel all around the world alone?

    B: Yes, I'll travel by _____.

2 A: I haven't seen you for a long time.

    B: Yes, long time _____ _____.

3 A: Can I have your car key, please?

    B: Yes, _____ it is.

4 A: Your report is great. You did a great _____!

    B: That's very nice of you to say so.

5 A: I did poorly on the final test.

    B: You _____ have studied harder.

1 다음을 듣고, 그림을 가장 적절하게 묘사한 것을 고르시오.

①   ②   ③   ④

2 다음을 듣고, 최근의 기상 상황을 바르게 나타낸 것을 고르시오.

① 폭염   ② 폭설
③ 폭우   ④ 태풍

3 대화를 듣고, 남자가 여자에게 부탁하는 일을 고르시오.

① 역사책을 읽어달라고
② 대신 필기를 해달라고
③ 필기한 것을 빌려달라고
④ 필기를 깨끗이 해달라고

4 대화를 듣고, 주말에 남자가 한 일을 고르시오.

① 축구시합을 했다.
② 컴퓨터로 축구게임을 했다.
③ TV로 축구경기를 시청했다.
④ 경기장에서 축구시합을 보았다.

5 다음을 듣고, 무엇에 관한 내용인지 고르시오.

① 관광 명소 소개
② 현장 학습 보고
③ 수학 여행 안내
④ 경주의 문화재 홍보

6 대화를 듣고, 남자의 직업으로 알맞은 것을 고르시오.

① poet   ② novelist
③ journalist   ④ scenarist

7 다음을 듣고, 두 사람의 대화가 <u>어색한</u> 것을 고르시오.

①   ②   ③   ④

8 대화를 듣고, 여자가 남자에게 전화를 건 목적을 고르시오.

① 약속날짜를 변경하려고
② 좀 늦을 것을 알려주려고
③ 언제 도착하는지 물어보려고
④ 약속시간이 언제인지 물어보려고

9 다음을 듣고, 여자가 말하고자 하는 속담으로 알맞은 것을 고르시오.

① Beauty is in the eye of the beholder.
② Beauty is only skin deep.
③ Honesty is the best policy.
④ Don't judge a book by its cover.

10 대화를 듣고, 운동장에 많이 있는 것으로 알맞은 것을 고르시오.

① 과자봉지   ② 잔디
③ 종이   ④ 공

11 대화를 듣고, Lucy의 모습으로 알맞은 것을 고르시오.

①   ②

③   ④

12 다음을 듣고, 무엇에 관한 내용인지 고르시오.

① 영어 회화 시험 안내
② 영어 회화 동아리 소개
③ 영어 회화 실력 향상법 소개
④ 영어 회화 학원 프로그램 안내

13 다음을 듣고, 주어진 상황에서 할 수 있는 말로 가장 적절한 것을 고르시오.

① May I take your order?
② Please sit down right here.
③ I'll be back with your food.
④ Your order will be ready soon.

14 다음을 듣고, 도표의 내용과 일치하지 <u>않는</u> 것을 고르시오.

Age	Total number of volunteers (thousands)	Average annual hours per person
16~24	7,798	40
25~34	9,019	36
35~44	12,902	52
45~54	13,136	55
55~64	9,316	60
65 and over	8,667	96

① ② ③ ④

15 대화를 듣고, 이번 학기가 끝나는 날짜를 고르시오.

① 7월 16일 ② 7월 19일
③ 7월 20일 ④ 7월 23일

16 대화를 듣고, 남자가 자기 방 청소를 하는 이유를 고르시오.

① 엄마한테 혼날까봐
② 방이 너무 지저분해서
③ 저녁때 나가서 놀려고
④ 여자와 숙제를 같이 하려고

17 대화를 듣고, 여자가 찾아가고자 하는 곳을 지도에서 고르시오.

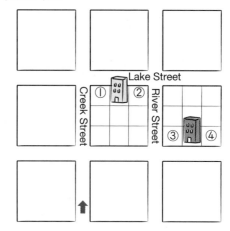

18 대화를 듣고, 남자의 기분으로 알맞은 것을 고르시오.

① scared ② thankful
③ bothered ④ sorry

[19-20] 대화를 듣고, 여자의 마지막 말에 이어질 남자의 응답으로 가장 적절한 것을 고르시오.

19

① At the subway station at 9 a.m.
② The tickets are expensive.
③ Meet me at 10 in the morning.
④ Sounds great. See you then.

20

① That's terrible news.
② The country is very safe.
③ I hope he has a good trip.
④ Your family must be happy.

1 다음을 듣고, 그림을 가장 적절하게 묘사한 것을 고르시오.

① ② ③ ④

M ① A teacher is writing _____ _____ _____.

② A teacher and a student are standing in front of the class.

③ A teacher is writing in _____ _____ _____.

④ A student is _____ _____ _____ to ask a teacher a question.

2 다음을 듣고, 최근의 기상 상황을 바르게 나타낸 것을 고르시오.

① 폭염
② 폭설
③ 폭우
④ 태풍

W Attention, listeners. Route 45 over the mountains is closed because of 25 cm _____ _____ _____. While the wind is not severe, _____ _____ _____ _____ _____ and the roads are becoming very icy. _____ _____ _____ _____ _____. But it is going to take a couple of days. So the Highway Department is closing Route 45.

3 대화를 듣고, 남자가 여자에게 부탁하는 일을 고르시오.

① 역사책을 읽어달라고
② 대신 필기를 해달라고
③ 필기한 것을 빌려달라고
④ 필기를 깨끗이 해달라고

M I need your help, Jenny.

W How can I help you?

M We have _____ _____ _____ tomorrow. But I cannot read my history notes.

W Why is that?

M As _____ _____ _____ _____, I couldn't write them down well.

W Oh, you said to me that you got your little finger stuck _____ _____ _____ _____. You must be careful.

M I will. But can I read your history notes?

W Yes, you can. But _____ _____ _____ _____.

4 대화를 듣고, 주말에 남자가 한 일을 고르시오.

① 축구시합을 했다.
② 컴퓨터로 축구게임을 했다.
③ TV로 축구경기를 시청했다.
④ 경기장에서 축구시합을 보았다.

W Did you watch the soccer game on the weekend?
M _____, _____ _____.
W It was a great game.
M I couldn't watch it. _____ _____ _____ _____ with my friends at that time.
W Oh, _____ _____ _____ _____, too?
M No, we lost. But it was _____ _____ _____.

5 다음을 듣고, 무엇에 관한 내용인지 고르시오.

① 관광 명소 소개
② 현장 학습 보고
③ 수학 여행 안내
④ 경주의 문화재 홍보

M Our school field trip was very good. Everyone got on the bus early in the morning. We drove _____ _____ _____ to Gyeongju. We visited a museum _____ _____ _____. We also saw a famous statue. It was my first time to _____ _____ _____. I learned many things about Korean history.

6 대화를 듣고, 남자의 직업으로 알맞은 것을 고르시오.

① poet
② novelist
③ journalist
④ scenarist

W Dad, what did you want to be when you were a child?
M _____ _____. As I was a child, I liked writing.
W Well, you aren't a journalist, but you still write.
M Yes, I do. I write _____ _____.
W And a journalist writes true stories.
M That's right. And I am happy to write stories _____ _____ _____.

7 다음을 듣고, 두 사람의 대화가 <u>어색한</u> 것을 고르시오.

①   ②   ③   ④

① **W** I'm worried about my English test.
   M Don't worry. _____ _____ _____ _____.
② **W** I'm going to see John tonight.
   M Tell him _____ _____ _____.
③ **W** Dad, I can't find my school bag.
   M _____ _____ _____ in the corner.
④ **W** I have good news.
   M I read about it _____ _____ _____.

8 대화를 듣고, 여자가 남자에게 전화를 건 목적을 고르시오.

① 약속날짜를 변경하려고
② 좀 늦을 것을 알려주려고
③ 언제 도착하는지 물어보려고
④ 약속시간이 언제인지 물어보려고

[Cell phone rings.]

M Hello.

W Michael, it's me.

M Oh, hi, Jennifer. Are you coming now? Is something wrong?

W Well, I'm going to _____ _____ _____ _____.

M It's 10 to 4 now. So when will you be here?

W I will be _____ _____ _____ _____.

M OK. _____ _____. Thanks for calling to tell me.

---

9 다음을 듣고, 여자가 말하고자 하는 속담으로 알맞은 것을 고르시오.

① Beauty is in the eye of the beholder.
② Beauty is only skin deep.
③ Honesty is the best policy.
④ Don't judgé a book by its cover.

W Everyone wants to look like a movie star. But this is not important. _____ _____ _____ is more important. If you are really cute but you are not a nice person, people will not want to be your friend. People think too much about _____ _____ _____. People should know there are more important things _____ _____.

---

10 대화를 듣고, 운동장에 많이 있는 것으로 알맞은 것을 고르시오.

① 과자봉지
② 잔디
③ 종이
④ 공

M Students throw their garbage _____ _____ _____ _____.

W Yes, they do. It's not good.

M There are _____ _____ _____ and cans of pop everywhere.

W Let's put them in the trash can. And we have to teach our students not to _____ _____ _____ _____.

M Also, I'll ask the principal to put more garbage cans outside.

---

11 대화를 듣고, Lucy의 모습으로 알맞은 것을 고르시오.

① ② ③ ④

M Oh, there is Lucy. I should go and say 'hello.'

W The girl you told me last time? Which one is Lucy?

M She has long hair.

W _____ _____ _____?

M She used to have straight hair, but she went to the beauty shop and _____ _____ _____ a few days ago.

W _____ _____ _____. OK. I see her.

12 다음을 듣고, 무엇에 관한 내용인지 고르시오.

① 영어 회화 시험 안내
② 영어 회화 동아리 소개
③ 영어 회화 실력 향상법 소개
④ 영어 회화 학원 프로그램 안내

M The English Conversation Club will meet _____ _____ _____ on Saturday afternoons. Any student can _____ _____ _____. The only rule is that _____ _____ _____ _____. If you have problems speaking English, don't worry. The other students and the teacher will help you. Please _____ _____ _____ your English speaking ability.

13 다음을 듣고, 주어진 상황에서 할 수 있는 말로 가장 적절한 것을 고르시오.

① May I take your order?
② Please sit down right here.
③ I'll be back with your food.
④ Your order will be ready soon.

W Mina has a new job in a restaurant. _____ _____ _____ _____. Two customers come into the restaurant. They sit down. A waiter _____ _____ _____ _____. After a few minutes, Mina goes over _____ _____ _____. She wants to know if they are ready to order. What is she likely to say to them?

14 다음을 듣고, 도표의 내용과 일치하지 <u>않는</u> 것을 고르시오.

Age	Total number of volunteers (thousands)	Average annual hours per person
16~24	7,798	40
25~34	9,019	36
35~44	12,902	52
45~54	13,136	55
55~64	9,316	60
65 and over	8,667	96

① ② ③ ④

M ① The greatest number of volunteers are 45 to 54 years old.
② People 65 years and older volunteer for more hours than _____ _____ _____ _____.
③ People 16 to 24 years old _____ _____ _____ _____ a year than people 25 to 34 years old.
④ _____ _____ _____ _____ volunteers are 16 to 24 years old.

15 대화를 듣고, 이번 학기가 끝나는 날짜를 고르시오.

① 7월 16일
② 7월 19일
③ 7월 20일
④ 7월 23일

M What day will school finish _____ _____?

W July 16th.

M Isn't it the day _____ _____ _____ _____?

W Oh, you're right. The last day of class is _____ _____ _____ _____.

M Are you sure? I thought it was the 23rd.

W No, school will start again on August 23rd.

M I see. Then I can go to sea on the 20th, the next day _____ _____ _____ _____.

16 대화를 듣고, 남자가 자기 방 청소를 하는 이유를 고르시오.

① 엄마한테 혼날까봐
② 방이 너무 지저분해서
③ 저녁때 나가서 놀려고
④ 여자와 숙제를 같이 하려고

W Wow! You're cleaning your room.

M Mom said I must clean my room. If I don't, _____ _____ _____ _____.

W You are cleaning so you can go out tonight.

M Yes, I want to meet my friends and _____ _____ _____.

W Mom has _____ _____ _____ _____ _____ you clean your room.

M That's right. Could you give me some help?

W Sorry, I have to study. I have lots of homework.

17 대화를 듣고, 여자가 찾아가고자 하는 곳을 지도에서 고르시오.

W Excuse me. Where is the Lake hospital?

M Lake hospital?

W Yes, how do I get to the hospital?

M _____ _____ _____ _____ and turn right. Then walk for one more block. _____ _____ _____ _____ of Lake and River Streets.

W Walk for two blocks _____ _____ _____. Walk to the corner of Lake and River Streets.

M Yes, _____ _____. It's next to a bank.

W Thank you.

18 대화를 듣고, 남자의 기분으로 알맞은 것을 고르시오.

① scared
② thankful
③ bothered
④ sorry

M Amy, I can't study because of you.

W Why?

M You're making _____ _____ _____ _____ .

W But we have something to talk about _____ _____ _____ . Wait for a moment. I will _____ _____ with Jason soon.

M Please _____ _____ _____ if you don't want to study right now.

---

19 대화를 듣고, 여자의 마지막 말에 이어질 남자의 응답으로 가장 적절한 것을 고르시오.

① At the subway station at 9 a.m.
② The tickets are expensive.
③ Meet me at 10 in the morning.
④ Sounds great. See you then.

M Where will we go tomorrow? Do you want to go _____ _____ _____ _____ ?

W Yes, that sounds like _____ _____ _____ .

M _____ _____ _____ , so we can have some fun.

W We can go on _____ _____ _____ .

M Yes, I love the Viking.

W Me too. Where do you want to meet?

M _____

---

20 대화를 듣고, 여자의 마지막 말에 이어질 남자의 응답으로 가장 적절한 것을 고르시오.

① That's terrible news.
② The country is very safe.
③ I hope he has a good trip.
④ Your family must be happy.

W My big brother is _____ _____ _____ _____ next week.

M Oh, when was the last time you saw him?

W Four or five months ago. My family went to _____ _____ _____ to see him.

M That's not _____ _____ _____ .

W This time he is _____ _____ _____ . He doesn't have to go back to the army.

M _____

1 다음을 듣고, 학생의 잘못으로 알맞은 것을 고르시오.

① 횡단보도가 아닌 곳에서 길을 건넜다.
② 자전거로 사람을 치었다.
③ 차에 색연필로 낙서를 했다.
④ 빨간 불에 길을 건넜다.

2 대화를 듣고, 두 사람의 관계로 알맞은 것을 고르시오.

① 엄마 - 아들
② 교사 - 학생
③ 학부모 - 교사
④ 학생 - 심사위원

3 다음을 듣고, 주어진 상황에서 할 수 있는 말로 적절한 것을 고르시오.

① Can you be quiet, please?
② You should be more careful.
③ I can't hear what you're saying.
④ Are you talking to me?

4 대화를 듣고, 남자가 병원에 가는 이유로 알맞은 것을 고르시오.

① 몸이 아파서
② 예방주사 맞으러
③ 병 문안하러
④ 정기검진 받으러

5 대화를 듣고, 남자가 사는 곳을 고르시오.

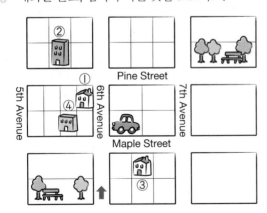

6 대화를 듣고, 컴퓨터에 무슨 문제가 있는지 고르시오.

① 모니터 고장
② 마우스 고장
③ 키보드 고장
④ 컴퓨터 바이러스

7 대화를 듣고, 여자가 전화를 한 목적을 고르시오.

① 예약 취소
② 식당 예약
③ 예약 시간 변경
④ 예약 날짜 변경

8 대화를 듣고, 엄마의 생신이 며칠인지 고르시오.

① 10일
② 12일
③ 13일
④ 14일

9 대화를 듣고, 지난 토요일에 남자가 한 일이 <u>아닌</u> 것을 고르시오.

① 집 청소
② 용돈 타기
③ 공원 가기
④ 영화 보러 가기

10 다음을 듣고, 두 사람의 대화가 <u>어색한</u> 것을 고르시오.
①   ②   ③   ④

11 대화를 듣고, 두 사람이 같이 스키를 타기로 한 날을 고르시오.

| JANUARY | | | | | | |
SUN	MON	TUE	WED	THU	FRI	SAT
				1	2	3
4	5	6	7	8	9	10
11	12	13	14	15	16	17
18	19	20	21	22	23	24
25	26	27	28	29	30	31

① 10일 　　　　　 ② 10~11일
③ 17일 　　　　　 ④ 17~18일

12 대화를 듣고, 남자가 거스름돈으로 받을 금액을 고르시오.

① 10 cents 　　　　 ② 20 cents
③ 60 cents 　　　　 ④ 1 dollar

13 대화를 듣고, 두 사람의 심정으로 알맞은 것을 고르시오.

① 따분한 　　　　 ② 화가 난
③ 만족스러운 　　 ④ 걱정스러운

14 대화를 듣고, 대화가 이루어지는 장소로 알맞은 것을 고르시오.

① airplane 　　　　 ② taxi
③ airport 　　　　 ④ coffee shop

15 대화를 듣고, 남자가 여자에게 하라고 하는 것을 고르시오.

① 수학 문제 풀기 　　 ② 퀴즈 문제 만들기
③ 시청 소감 보내기 　 ④ 퀴즈 대회 참가

16 다음을 듣고, 그림의 상황에 가장 알맞은 대화를 고르시오.

① 　　　 ② 　　　 ③ 　　　 ④

17 대화를 듣고, 두 사람의 관계로 알맞은 것을 고르시오.

① 범인 – 변호사
② 시민 – 경찰
③ 은행원 – 고객
④ 사진작가 – 모델

18 대화를 듣고, 대화의 내용과 일치하는 것을 고르시오.

① 남자는 숙제를 하지 않았다.
② 여자는 남자에게 숙제를 보여주었다.
③ 남자는 여자의 숙제를 베끼지 않았다.
④ 여자는 남자에게 풀이 방법을 가르쳐줬다.

[19-20] 대화를 듣고, 남자의 마지막 말에 이어질 여자의 응답으로 가장 적절한 것을 고르시오.

19

① One moment. I will correct the bill.
② Please pay at the receptionist desk.
③ OK. Everything is correct on the bill.
④ Los Angeles is much warmer than Toronto.

20

① Happy birthday to you!
② Maybe some other time.
③ I'll see you this weekend.
④ The weather will be sunny.

1 다음을 듣고, 학생의 잘못으로 알맞은 것을 고르시오.

① 횡단보도가 아닌 곳에서 길을 건넜다.
② 자전거로 사람을 치었다.
③ 차에 색연필로 낙서를 했다.
④ 빨간 불에 길을 건넜다.

M Attention, students. There was an accident in front of the school yesterday. A car hit a student. _____ _____ _____ _____ _____. The student was crossing the street _____ _____ _____ _____. Please don't do this. You must always wait for a green light. You must be always careful _____ _____ _____ _____ near the school.

2 대화를 듣고, 두 사람의 관계로 알맞은 것을 고르시오.

① 엄마 – 아들
② 교사 – 학생
③ 학부모 – 교사
④ 학생 – 심사위원

M Excuse me, Mrs. Lee. I have heard there will be a writing contest next month. Can I enter _____ _____ _____ _____?
W Yes, you can. Your writing _____ _____ _____ is very good.
M Thank you. Can I have the information paper?
W _____ _____ _____. Good luck to you.
M Bye. See you in class _____ _____.

3 다음을 듣고, 주어진 상황에서 할 수 있는 말로 적절한 것을 고르시오.

① Can you be quiet, please?
② You should be more careful.
③ I can't hear what you're saying.
④ Are you talking to me?

M You are studying in the library. You have an important test next week. Some other students _____ _____ _____ _____. They are talking and using their cell phone. You want to _____ _____ _____ _____ _____ so much noise. In this situation, what would you say to them?

4 대화를 듣고, 남자가 병원에 가는 이유로 알맞은 것을 고르시오.

① 몸이 아파서
② 예방주사 맞으러
③ 병 문안하러
④ 정기검진 받으러

M Hi, Jenny. _____ _____ I have to cancel our appointment. I'm going to the doctor's this weekend.
W Why? Are you sick? Or are you going to see a person in the hospital?
M No, I have to have _____ _____ _____. But I forgot.
W Is it just a checkup?
M Yes, _____ _____ _____ I am in good health. I think regular checkups are _____ _____ _____ in maintaining good health.

5 대화를 듣고, 남자가 사는 곳을 고르시오.

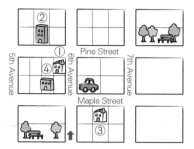

M Next Saturday is my birthday. Would you _____ _____ _____ _____ ? Some other friends will come, too.

W OK. _____ _____ _____ _____ . By the way, where do you live?

M I live on Maple Street.

W Where on Maple Street?

M I live _____ _____ _____ _____ Avenues.

W Between 5th and 6th Avenues.

M Yes, I live _____ _____ _____ _____ .

W I can find your house easily.

6 대화를 듣고, 컴퓨터에 무슨 문제가 있는지 고르시오.

① 모니터 고장
② 마우스 고장
③ 키보드 고장
④ 컴퓨터 바이러스

M It's not a computer virus, Beth.

W But _____ _____ _____ . It wasn't working properly.

M Well, the problem is your keyboard. Did you _____ _____ _____ _____ ?

W Umm... Maybe some coffee yesterday.

M Well, that's probably the reason it doesn't work. _____ _____ _____ _____ . The monitor is fine. But you do need _____ _____ _____ .

7 대화를 듣고, 여자가 전화를 한 목적을 고르시오.

① 예약 취소
② 식당 예약
③ 예약 시간 변경
④ 예약 날짜 변경

[Telephone rings.]

M Hello. John's BBQ Ribs Restaurant.

W Hello. I'd like to make a reservation.

M _____ _____ _____ ?

W Tonight.

M For what time?

W 6 p.m. for four people. Do you have _____ _____ _____ ?

M Well, can you come later?

W Yes, _____ _____ _____ ?

M At 7.

W Yes, _____ _____ _____ . My name is Sally Swanson.

M See you then, Ms. Swanson.

8 대화를 듣고, 엄마의 생신이 며칠인지 고르시오.

① 10일
② 12일
③ 13일
④ 14일

M What's the date today?

W _____ _____ . It's Tuesday the 10th of June.

M Isn't it Mom's birthday?

W No, it's not. Her birthday is _____ _____ _____ .

M _____ _____ _____ ?

W No, Thursday is the 12th not the 13th. Have you bought a present for mom? I have a good idea _____ _____ _____ .

9 대화를 듣고, 지난 토요일에 남자가 한 일이 아닌 것을 고르시오.

① 집 청소
② 용돈 타기
③ 공원 가기
④ 영화 보러 가기

W What did you do last weekend?

M I cleaned the house last Saturday afternoon.

W Oh, that doesn't sound like fun. _____ _____ _____ ?

M Well, after I cleaned the house, I _____ _____ _____ from my dad. Then I could _____ _____ _____ _____ with my friends.

W _____ _____ _____ _____ ?

M Yes. How about you?

W I went to the park with my family.

10 다음을 듣고, 두 사람의 대화가 어색한 것을 고르시오.

①   ②   ③   ④

① W Are you going to _____ _____ _____ ?
    M Yes, _____ _____ we meet again this weekend.

② W I _____ _____ _____ in the English speaking contest.
    M I'm sorry to hear that. You will do better next time.

③ W Excuse me, I'd like to buy some flowers.
    M _____ _____ do you like?

④ W _____ _____ _____ last night?
    M At my friend's house. I helped my friend with his homework.

11 대화를 듣고, 두 사람이 같이 스키를 타기로 한 날을 고르시오.

JANUARY

SUN	MON	TUE	WED	THU	FRI	SAT
				1	2	3
4	5	6	7	8	9	10
11	12	13	14	15	16	17
18	19	20	21	22	23	24
25	26	27	28	29	30	

① 10일
② 10~11일
③ 17일
④ 17~18일

M Let's go skiing in January.

W Good idea. How about _____ _____ _____ in January?

M OK. But can you _____ _____ _____ ?

W You mean both Saturday and Sunday?

M Yes, I do. I want to ski for _____ _____ _____

_____ .

W _____ , _____ _____ . I have something to do.

M OK. We can go again later this winter.

12 대화를 듣고, 남자가 거스름돈으로 받을 금액을 고르시오.

① 10 cents
② 20 cents
③ 60 cents
④ 1 dollar

W May I help you? What are you looking for?

M _____ _____ _____ _____ ?

W They are over here.

M Oh, thanks. I'll take this newspaper and the two packets of

_____ _____ .

W The newspaper is one dollar.

M And the gum?

W It's only _____ _____ _____ _____ .

M Here's a _____ _____ _____ .

W And here's your change.

13 대화를 듣고, 두 사람의 심정으로 알맞은 것을 고르시오.

① 따분한
② 화가 난
③ 만족스러운
④ 걱정스러운

M Where is our food?

W Yes, the food should be here already.

M We've been waiting 50 minutes!

W Yes, _____ _____ _____ .

M Twenty minutes ago, he said my steak would be a few minutes.

W I can't wait any more. _____ _____ _____ .

M _____ _____ _____ _____ . I will ask him one more time.

14 대화를 듣고, 대화가 이루어지는 장소로 알맞은 것을 고르시오.

① airplane
② taxi
③ airport
④ coffee shop

M _____ _____ _____ _____ late arriving.

W How do you know that?

M Yes, _____ _____. He is on flight AC 456.

W Yes. I see it.

M Well, it says the flight is 45 minutes _____ _____.

W Let's go and have a coffee then.

---

15 대화를 듣고, 남자가 여자에게 하라고 하는 것을 고르시오.

① 수학 문제 풀기
② 퀴즈 문제 만들기
③ 시청 소감 보내기
④ 퀴즈 대회 참가

M Wow! You answered to all the questions of this TV quiz show today.

W Yes, I do. The questions were easy today.

M You should _____ _____ _____ _____.

W _Quiz, Quiz_? You mean I should _____ _____ _____.

M Yes, you should go on the show and answer quiz questions.

W Well, I will find _____ _____ _____ to the quiz show.

M Good! If you go on the show, you will do well.

---

16 다음을 듣고, 그림의 상황에 가장 알맞은 대화를 고르시오.

① ② ③ ④

① **M** Well, Sophie, I have to leave now.

  W _____ _____ _____? It's not even 1:45.

② **M** Do you have _____ _____ for this summer?

  W Yeah, I'd like to read the books I've wanted to read.

③ **M** Good evening. I'd like to reserve a room for two.

  W Sure. _____ _____ _____ _____? A deluxe room or a suite?

④ **M** It's a _____ _____ of Shakespeare's _Othello_.

  W Wow! I like Shakespeare's plays.

---

17 대화를 듣고, 두 사람의 관계로 알맞은 것을 고르시오.

① 범인 – 변호사
② 시민 – 경찰
③ 은행원 – 고객
④ 사진작가 – 모델

M Are you OK? _____ _____ _____?

W No, not at all. I'm OK. But he took my handbag and ran. There is a lot of money in my handbag. _____ _____ _____ from this bank.

M What did he _____ _____?

W He was tall and thin. He was wearing jeans.

M Can you come down to the station to look at _____ _____ _____?

W Yes, I can.

18 대화를 듣고, 대화의 내용과 일치하는 것을 고르시오.

① 남자는 숙제를 하지 않았다.
② 여자는 남자에게 숙제를 보여주었다.
③ 남자는 여자의 숙제를 베끼지 않았다.
④ 여자는 남자에게 풀이 방법을 가르쳐줬다.

M Can I see your homework?

W My homework? _____ _____ _____ my homework.

M I don't want _____ _____ _____.

W Really? Why do you want to see mine?

M I want to check if I _____ _____ _____ _____. Or would you tell me the numbers?

W You had to do questions 1, 2 and 3 for homework.

M Thank you.

---

19 대화를 듣고, 남자의 마지막 말에 이어질 여자의 응답으로 가장 적절한 것을 고르시오.

① One moment. I will correct the bill.
② Please pay at the receptionist desk.
③ OK. Everything is correct on the bill.
④ Los Angeles is much warmer than Toronto.

M Excuse me, there is a mistake _____ _____ _____.

W Really? What is the mistake?

M Well, I stayed in the hotel three _____ _____ _____.

W Oh, that's right.

M There was _____ _____ _____ in Toronto and I arrived in Los Angeles one day late. And I told you on the phone before I arrived here.

W Yes, you're right. _____ _____ _____.

M Can you correct the bill?

W _____

---

20 대화를 듣고, 남자의 마지막 말에 이어질 여자의 응답으로 가장 적절한 것을 고르시오.

① Happy birthday to you!
② Maybe some other time.
③ I'll see you this weekend.
④ The weather will be sunny.

W Can you go with me to the beach this weekend?

M Oh, _____ _____ _____, but I can't.

W Are you busy?

M Yes, it's my grandmother's birthday. Our family _____ _____ _____ at an Italian restaurant.

W Oh, that's great. I hope _____ _____ _____ _____ at the party.

M Thank you. I'm sorry _____ _____ with you.

W _____

A Write down the definition of each word or phrase.

1	raise	11	have fun
2	attention	12	period
3	severe	13	yearly
4	statue	14	tool
5	fiction	15	properly
6	personality	16	bill
7	appearance	17	contestant
8	policy	18	reserve
9	ability	19	withdraw
10	semester	20	receptionist

B Match each word with the right definition.

1	pop	_____	a	보도기자, 신문(잡지) 기자, 언론인
2	maintain	_____	b	판단하다
3	duty	_____	c	탄산음료
4	checkup	_____	d	쓰레기통
5	behind schedule	_____	e	~에 도착하다
6	make sure	_____	f	돌아가(오)다
7	trash can	_____	g	의무, 임무
8	correct	_____	h	건강진단
9	spill	_____	i	확인(확신)하다, 반드시 ~하다
10	judge	_____	j	귀중한, 소중한
11	valuable	_____	k	유지하다
12	journalist	_____	l	엎지르다, 흘리다
13	return	_____	m	거스름돈, 잔돈
14	get to	_____	n	예정보다 늦게
15	change	_____	o	정정하다, 고치다; 옳은, 정확한

C Choose the best answer for the blank.

1 It is going to take a _____ of days.

a. pair b. piece c. couple

2 You _____ that story, didn't you?

a. made up b. made of c. made out

3 I saw you _____ the bus going downtown.

a. take on b. get on c. ride on

4 Speak loudly _____ everyone can hear.

a. as that b. so that c. now that

5 She asked me _____ I wanted some more rice.

a. if b. that c. what

6 Can you have a look at my computer? It doesn't _____ properly.

a. move b. go c. work

D Complete the short dialogues.

1 A: What's the _____ today?

B: It's June 10th.

2 A: What do you do to maintain your health?

B: Exercise! It keeps me _____ good health.

3 A: Where do you live?

B: I live _____ 5th and 6th Avenues.

4 A: Can you be quiet, please?

B: I'm sorry to _____ so much noise.

5 A: What did your doctor say?

B: He suggested that I _____ a walk every day.

위아

중학듣기
모의고사

2

정답

영어듣기능력평가 • 1회

1	2	3	4	5	6	7	8	9	10
④	③	③	②	④	①	④	②	②	①

11	12	13	14	15	16	17	18	19	20
③	①	②	③	②	②	③	②	④	①

1 with regular gas / Fill it up / give me a ride / Was I speeding

2 will be held / enter the talent show / play a musical instrument

3 on the table / put the side dishes / in her room / come and eat

4 I have done it / released yet / take a walk

5 get to work / I didn't drive / the safest and fastest

6 That sounds interesting / borrow any books / check it out

7 Which movie / I had enough / If you don't mind

8 Slow down / put up new signs / in a school zone

9 I'm interested in / too much pollution / live safely

10 already bought one / pens and pencils / giving a concert

11 That's amazing / at least one instrument / try the cello / some basic skills

12 you can't go out / That is why / Take a rest

13 help the old people / So I volunteered / clean their rooms

14 in my studies / You'll have to stop / at all / should spend less time

15 at the library / You only have 20 minutes / I might have to leave

16 You look worried / to hear that / he has many problems

17 When did she move / She is living with / Just one

18 experienced different weather / the south will be sunny / enjoy warm weather

19 I'm very tired / for 4   hours straight / have a drink

20 won the writing contest / spent a lot of time

영어듣기능력평가 • 2회

1	2	3	4	5	6	7	8	9	10
②	②	①	③	③	④	②	①	③	①

11	12	13	14	15	16	17	18	19	20
③	②	②	④	②	③	②	④	③	④

1 are not healthy / they stay over night / the doctors let them leave

2 for exercise / I don't like to sweat / I go for a walk

3 He acts like me / be a police officer / while I prefer / That's the only difference

4 10 degrees outside / warm but windy / will be thankful

5 Biology / get good grades / in a space station

6 I don't have / play board games / my family would do that

7 this striped shirt / my favorite pattern / out of fashion / Checkers are OK

8 That's too often / just have a drink / In addition

9 I'm going out / get a library book / take a book back

10 will the repairperson / We're very busy / over this evening

11 not as popular as / like fresh fruit / Five students

12 twice a week / perfect for a picnic / I did poorly / Cheer up

13 The meals include drinks / $4 each / get one for free

14 reserved a table / Follow me / Enjoy your meal

15 is sold out / the last show / Can we drive to / It's near here

16 I bought you / in that pink shirt / I'm not very comfortable / wear my jacket

17 I'll be moving out / inviting me / across town / We're about to close

18 bought your present / let you know / Give me a hint

19 Who is it / In the playground / just in front of

20 in your party / Two adults / a table available

1	2	3	4	5	6	7	8	9	10
①	④	②	③	③	①	①	④	③	③

11	12	13	14	15	16	17	18	19	20
②	③	①	③	③	②	②	①	③	④

1 Half past three / board the plane / Please watch out / Our luggage / have a watch

2 skin cancer / you shouldn't stay / The summer sun

3 we have to do / not good at that / vacuum the floor

4 She is getting better / she hurt her arm / to cheer her up

5 the way that things are / Not really / more than science

6 Coke or sprite / That's correct / this coupon / save one dollar

7 How much milk / What about you / On the next block

8 turn off the lights / save electricity / We can't waste it

9 that involves cars / fixing broken car / be a mechanic / racing driver

10 he would write / only wrote once / On the other hand / so easily discarded

11 high up on trees / have dark spots / King of the Jungle

12 have an emergency / in pain / broke a tooth

13 find a day / Saturday afternoon / Let's meet then

14 I just fell down / I'm assuming / perfectly the first time

15 It takes too long / an hour and 45 minutes / take the express bus

16 a storm is coming up / stay home / might be terrible

17 such a long time / your classmate / talking about clothes / That's not true

18 It was very cold / tomorrow will be snowy / Remember to dress

19 have any plans / in the countryside / She'll be happy

20 Where are you from / a few years ago / What part of

1	2	3	4	5	6	7	8	9	10
②	②	①	②	①	②	④	①	③	②

11	12	13	14	15	16	17	18	19	20
④	③	②	②	②	④	②	②	①	①

1 chasing another boy / watching a soccer game / walking down

2 Look outside / It started snowing / Call your child's school

3 cost per hour / park your car for / Here is a ticket / lock your car

4 couldn't rent any / take a walk / went in-line skating

5 For one hour / All brands of sunglasses / the first floor

6 ever sit down / grow plants / raise a crop

7 I'm a moviegoer / I'm very grateful / You look worried

8 A lot better / You missed three days / I will be there

9 prepared himself / He wrote an essay / he had studied

10 The main act / perform a few songs / is not well-known here

11 do you prefer / Take a guess / Rice cake / the next layer

12 on your knowledge / bring it to me / the bell rings / Be quiet

13 in her room / go and get her / the person to wait

14 by one year / lightest, and shortest / among the three

15 we have to be / start dinner around 8 / leave right away / 30 minutes

16 have a bad cold / take some vitamins / at the pharmacy

17 ten students like / the least favorite subject / Math is as popular as

18 lie on the sofa / Kind of / I needed some rest / go away

19 Today's special is salmon / very popular dish

20 the kitchen cupboard / on the top shelf / stand on a chair

영어듣기능력평가 • 5회

1	2	3	4	5	6	7	8	9	10
③	②	④	②	①	③	②	④	③	④

11	12	13	14	15	16	17	18	19	20
③	③	②	①	④	④	①	④	①	③

1   Every student brought / built a cake / The funny thing / didn't eat any

2   my second movie / the main character / from the director / must have been great

3   the sixth largest / is surrounded by water / It is a continent / dry desert

4   let's not bother her / much taller than / could be an actress

5   I was thinking I'm lost / go across the street / It's on the left side

6   watching my weight currently / any diet coke / try to avoid / make some tea

7   Why haven't you come / for 30 minutes more / But that's it

8   born in December / three months older / on the 5th of September

9   exchange some money / It's time to check-in / Wheel the cart

10 My dog died / me to come over / rush hour traffic

11 take you out / the third Monday / get paid on the 20th / treat for me

12 in my wallet / It has expired / had an expiration date

13 I'm almost finished / I don't care / turn it off right now

14 make a deposit / fill out this form / account book

15 Can you come to / lots of things to carry / I'll be there

16 The weather seems good / let me put on / you're into biking / your steak done / for the picnic

17 the most valuable player / It's an honor / tell the viewers / I turned and shot quickly

18 solve question / how to do it / Are you having trouble

19 go to a concert / all sold out / an extra ticket

20 You sound like / I can't stop coughing / to get some rest

영어듣기능력평가 • 6회

1	2	3	4	5	6	7	8	9	10
②	③	①	④	③	①	③	④	①	②

11	12	13	14	15	16	17	18	19	20
②	②	③	②	③	④	④	②	③	④

1   Which cookies / I baked them / be ready soon / Don't eat snacks

2   in order / get on first / are sitting in rows / boarding pass ready

3   develop this film / That's fast / maybe I will wait / I'll just look around

4   see them a lot / four times a week / brings it over

5   the sports section / the local news / the international news first

6   This painting / it was painted / this exhibit / only be here

7   that guy over there / the same elementary school / You are so kind / I walk to school

8   will start shortly / throughout the zoo / do not give food / get off the train

9   Is your job hard / a secret ingredient / try your food

10 just around the corner / Come with me / a good book

11 copies of photos / put the paper / press a button

12 some channels / Will you be home / Our repairperson

13 what I told you / no television / I'll just read / that are on the table

14 looks delicious / better than my seafood rice / some more of mine

15 It may be faster / When do they leave / an hour and 15 minutes

16 Our study team / keep your promise / let it happen again

17 are destroyed / is damaged / can't talk to you / they won't worry

18 be cold and rainy / even though it's not sunny / until the weekend arrives

19 by that name / the Smith household / want to call

20 I was stuck / you finally made it / Where should I

1	2	3	4	5	6	7	8	9	10
①	③	①	④	②	③	②	①	④	④

11	12	13	14	15	16	17	18	19	20
②	④	③	③	②	④	③	③	①	①

1 use these to listen / portable media player / go over your head

2 misses her family / with a backpack / she stays in hotels

3 go to the hospital / had an operation / bring him some juice

4 no rain or wind / move out tomorrow

5 feed the animals / that's the part of my job / the animals' cages

6 tend to be hungry / I only eat cereal / eat a bigger breakfast

7 take a long time / No left turns / on the next street

8 for parents' day / my dad a necktie / spend any money / saved my allowance

9 That's not enough time / after the show / to look at

10 About an hour / the last subway / had better hurry

11 a buffet restaurant / open every day / don't have to make

12 makes me laugh / I need your help / think of this novel

13 $35 / The round trip / two one-way tickets

14 reserved a double room / does the room cost / I have a headache

15 play volleyball first / cool down in the ocean / get the ball

16 studied all night / My stomach is upset / worry about failing

17 on the poster / How cute / Who is this girl / an hour ago

18 find the piece / Puzzles should relax you / look for it anymore

19 she's not home / ask her to call

20 a nice party / become good friends / Before I forget

1	2	3	4	5	6	7	8	9	10
①	④	③	②	①	①	②	②	①	③

11	12	13	14	15	16	17	18	19	20
②	②	③	③	②	②	④	①	②	①

1 A clerk is helping / at a food stall

2 cool and cloudy / return in two / days fly a kite

3 a pair of pants / Over there / try them on

4 hike up the mountain / the rain to stop / on the bus / some students just slept

5 improve your vocabulary / in a story / without trying hard

6 be a guide / very inexpensively / meet various people

7 You're welcome. Anytime / any cake left / turn it down

8 studying and / working on hand it / See you

9 many different groups / who don't like sports / in each group / mainly who are like them

10 in a special notebook / is written down / to ask about homework

11 You look pale / cough and sneeze / a bad headache

12 both turned 60 / travel around the world / In the fall / they plan to go

13 lost a big game / He feels sad / make him feel better

14 each night / the latest / at the same time

15 by regular mail / take 2 days / an overnight service / by registered mail

16 early than usual / then the phone rang / a big problem

17 the most popular activity / play board games / more popular than

18 You did your best / cherish your advice / hardworking girl

19 may be important / I can't find / lend you a pencil

20 put on my sweater / why I was cold / to close it

1	2	3	4	5	6	7	8	9	10
④	②	②	③	③	②	①	②	④	④

11	12	13	14	15	16	17	18	19	20
③	②	④	④	①	④	④	③	④	②

1 bought some books / had some snacks / we didn't buy

2 make two copies / Will there be / buy this pen

3 He is nervous / He sounds good / he will win

4 for a walk / your aunt is visiting / scared of dogs

5 Walk two blocks / the second shop / past the hotel

6 I've gotten everything / get any cheese / wait in the line

7 that are overdue / bring them back / the latest movie

8 in four days / Yesterday was Sunday / I was wrong

9 you didn't answer / Did you meet her / I should have stayed home

10 the wrong bus / Help yourself / she look like / see you then

11 here is amazing / some orange juice / the cream cake

12 looking for a tie / it's on sale / I'll buy two then

13 for vacation / to take me there / It's not possible

14 a basket / very ripe right now / some mandarin oranges / where a flower shop

15 at night recently / have worries / take a bath / It will relax you

16 planning on going there / Please connect me / register a complaint

17 my prescription / Have you gotten / prepare your medicine

18 haven't even started / whose brother dies / a terrible disease / That sounds scary

19 favorite sport / you liked basketball / I saw her playing

20 fill out this form / date of birth / write down the month

1	2	3	4	5	6	7	8	9	10
③	②	③	③	①	④	①	④	②	④

11	12	13	14	15	16	17	18	19	20
③	③	②	③	③	②	③	②	①	①

1 recommend something delicious / clean up / carry the box

2 like rice and wheat / one serving a day

3 something unusual / from the pharmacy / the doctor's office

4 going to start soon / No, you can't / I'll do it

5 But I don't / those interview shows / any comedies on / turn the channel

6 here's the book / have enough money / looked for it

7 Personally I don't / on my way to school / on weekends

8 in a recycling bin / too many plastic bags / tell the shopkeeper

9 I give directions / you catch criminals / joining the force

10 I decided to lose weight / eating healthy food / not just say it

11 small and portable / put into a computer / keeps the information

12 take a bus home / Can't you pick me up / very sore currently

13 he's smart / talk a lot / he stayed at school / at home

14 any money left / half of my allowance / skipping your meals

15 should I meet you / The show doesn't start / I don't leave work

16 no fun / makes me feel sick / look out the window

17 Winter jackets / be in fashion / take that chance

18 It rained hard all day / as it was today / continue until the first

19 inviting me over / watch it together / make yourself at home

20 I'm in a hurry / return some books / No, I didn't

영어듣기능력평가 ● 11회

1	2	3	4	5	6	7	8	9	10
④	②	③	④	③	②	④	③	①	③

11	12	13	14	15	16	17	18	19	20
③	①	②	④	②	④	③	②	③	①

1 He lives close to / meets a friend / with her dad / bows politely

2 Was it the acting / a poor cartoon / the special effects

3 It is easier than / are hard to buy / clothing / agree with you more

4 do your homework / new notebooks and pens / make some food

5 in my class / She is considerate / be proud of her

6 working late again / haven't been home early

7 on his way home / He didn't buy any books / some pens and pencils

8 Instant noodles / put an egg / pieces of rice cake

9 Can I borrow / study the book / lend it to you

10 were driving / Isn't the speed limit / I didn't know that

11 the nearest bank / the second building / on my right

12 do me a favor / take an umbrella / Did you forget

13 sales taxes / the federal government / pay both taxes

14 draw and paint / playing sports / I dislike the most

15 It's too greasy / eat something healthier / eat Korean food

16 Someone is knocking / at this time / enter the house

17 you were admitted / I appreciate it / around a tooth / behind me

18 The game was tied / a penalty kick / illegal play / made a mistake

19 is absent from / Is he sick / a high temperature

20 hold the door open / carry one box / very heavy

영어듣기능력평가 ● 12회

1	2	3	4	5	6	7	8	9	10
①	③	①	②	④	④	①	②	②	③

11	12	13	14	15	16	17	18	19	20
②	①	③	④	③	②	③	③	③	①

1 in front of a theater / renting a movie / on a ride

2 used to take me / we'd have dinner / a lot of fun / we would read books

3 with the daily special / the mushroom soup / then I suggest / I'll have it

4 in the countryside / small vegetable garden / visit them often

5 I want to announce / on any topic / For more information

6 Math is important / helping others learn / do you like children

7 I'm so scared / keep your promise / forgive me

8 leave the station / once an hour / past the hour

9 shake my hand / I bowed instead / behave like

10 hot weather / lie in the sun having outdoor / barbecues

11 many rooms / business person travels / pay money to sleep

12 hearing problems / through earphones / keep the volume low

13 looks really sad / stay in the hospital / want to comfort him

14 Take off / backpack and hat / throw anything / under 12 years

15 on the 30th / it's the last day / many days to go

16 play any musical instrument / play the guitar / May I introduce

17 than the guitar / The same number / play the violin

18 hear me screaming / falling to the ground / It's exciting

19 Which concert / don't you / rock and roll music / not really

20 Do you have time / Romantic comedies / Love Actually

1	2	3	4	5	6	7	8	9	10
③	④	③	①	②	③	①	④	③	③

11	12	13	14	15	16	17	18	19	20
③	①	②	②	③	③	③	①	①	③

1 a great birthday party / the park and played / I was given

2 will be landing / sign is on / from the airport

3 walking toward the door / help her by holding

4 my hair cut short / I would look good / they might be right

5 near a bank / opposite the flower shop / not next to

6 I've been dieting / much better sense / some shirts and ties / if you'd come

7 Do you own / parked in front of / I can't move

8 the bus is quicker / take a subway / take much longer

9 a stressful weekend / got lost / soldiers carrying guns / I dropped off

10 for too long / it's hot but delicious / I'm so excited / wait for a moment

11 Two adult tickets / your youngest / you only need two

12 get two for free / I guess so / Take a tray

13 for breaking his watch / buy me a cell phone / be the only boy

14 in society / pollute the environment / drive smaller cars

15 study biology / I could decide / I am just suggesting / famous surgeon

16 resolve the issue / Get dressed quickly / you're so wet / I got stuck / I can drop by

17 about your education / any work experience / my first job

18 you would / rode my bike / I didn't see you / on Sunday

19 the perfect dessert / I'll be here soon / There is none left

20 too many pimples / Those are common / facial cleanser cream / some special soap

1	2	3	4	5	6	7	8	9	10
①	③	③	①	③	①	③	④	②	③

11	12	13	14	15	16	17	18	19	20
③	①	②	③	④	③	④	③	①	①

1 get caught / the most convenient time / It's my pleasure

2 starts to get colder / turn red / fall off

3 No, not yet / get lunch ready / any snacks / You ate them all

4 need a book / do my science homework / with my family

5 a good cook / A tuna sandwich / Your grandmother did / Good boy

6 clean the blackboard / plenty of chalk / clean the brushes

7 have a headache / Let's eat out / go to bed now

8 for so long / let you go / no tickets left / have no choice

9 Same size, same shape / design them / You're very creative

10 No, I forgot / you shouldn't talk / the day before yesterday / like the kitchen pot

11 the very first vehicle / one large wheel / in the back / pedal it to move

12 with some problems / study with me / explain things to me

13 A headache / It's really painful / My dentist

14 Excuse me / a smaller size / get my money back / have a receipt

15 Nice to hear / sixteen hours ahead / miss both of you

16 the book I lent you / I apologize / remember to bring it

17 celebrate Parents' Day / other small gifts / do special things / cook breakfast

18 bad storm / blow away / protect your plants

19 I'm really thirsty / juice and milk / What kind of

20 Can you meet me / do some shopping first / time to eat

영어듣기능력평가 ● 15회

1	2	3	4	5	6	7	8	9	10
③	①	③	③	①	①	②	②	③	①

11	12	13	14	15	16	17	18	19	20
④	①	②	①	②	①	④	③	①	②

1 While her mother cooked / in the living room / put the dishes

2 lose weight / as often as possible / walk up the stairs

3 eat breakfast / have some toast / with milk / for the brain

4 study at home / Not me / the best place / no TV set

5 do you go by / same bus stop / Just wait here

6 fighting and death / much violence / more educational

7 Take a guess / in a zigzag pattern / have poison

8 What's wrong / Look outside / I took mine / share yours

9 I washed them / They have a hole / I fell down

10 speak with / by that name / It's 936-2202

11 an only child / as many brothers as / has more sisters

12 taking a walk / get to the bakery / a great idea

13 buy this watch / the silver one / it's 30% off

14 One of my teeth / I shouldn't bite / broke your tooth / I'll prescribe

15 new clothes / so old-fashioned / for his birthday / let's do that

16 answers the door / for the first time / say to her

17 You performed very well / Is everything packed / mind having a look

18 front yard / I am frightened of / it barks loudly

19 nice talking to you / Are you going home / your sister doing

20 I can't decide / Medium rare, please / What kind of soup

영어듣기능력평가 ● 16회

1	2	3	4	5	6	7	8	9	10
②	③	④	③	②	③	④	④	②	④

11	12	13	14	15	16	17	18	19	20
③	②	①	④	②	②	③	③	②	②

1 A man is feeding / at a stranger / guides a blind man

2 kept in cages / should be free / space to run around

3 some running shoes / on good stuff / does it

4 played card games / Why didn't you come / help her with chores

5 social studies / Korean literature / The final two classes

6 to be successful / my clothes match / interesting patterns and prints

7 I dropped it / Which sport / fast and exciting / a good person

8 press the right button / the movies playing / the adventure film

9 shouldn't say bad things / walls which can hear

10 pork cutlets / She cooked it better / never say that

11 an insect / small head on top / red with black spots

12 stop you from studying / want to sing along / helps me concentrate

13 go downtown / give her a ride / she thanks you / would you reply

14 went on a picnic / went boating on a river / on the grass

15 had enough / leave a tip / pay for it

16 to learn English / visiting my relatives / About two weeks

17 Pardon me / the public library is / and turn right / It's next to / it's across the street

18 the last test scores / Not too bad / what I thought / You sound satisfied

19 Do you mean / you look better / care about the color

20 something to eat / I'm really hungry / Let's just get / in my wallet

정답 ● **197**

영어듣기능력평가 • 17회

1	2	3	4	5	6	7	8	9	10
③	③	①	④	④	②	②	④	③	④

11	12	13	14	15	16	17	18	19	20
④	①	③	④	②	④	①	④	①	①

1 have your attention / The librarian will be there / on the field trip

2 be a virus / and fix it / with the computer first / to my repair shop

3 his rice quickly / some more rice / He is not hungry

4 I have some stamps / got a notice / There is a parcel

5 on your right / walk two more blocks / in the middle of

6 a lot of errands / and the photo shop / when you get back

7 cancel your appointment / phone our office / to set up

8 to have meal / keep healthy snacks / if you eat better

9 Not last weekend / I took a rest / should be well prepared

10 in science / I'm very grateful / visit the palace / go there alone

11 right away / at the store / Then you cleaned / taking a break

12 are the cookies / help poor children / take two boxes

13 Quit changing channels / There is nothing on / Just keep it on

14 greatest spy / for the 10th movie

15 with a little honey / help my cold / made me chicken soup / It may work

16 drawing a picture of / I'm afraid I can't / Elephants cannot jump

17 in person / movie of mine / Can you sign

18 the whole time / I played by myself / I'm not lonely

19 It has many pieces / I almost gave up

20 You look upset / have trouble with / except for this question

영어듣기능력평가 • 18회

1	2	3	4	5	6	7	8	9	10
③	②	④	④	①	②	②	④	①	①

11	12	13	14	15	16	17	18	19	20
②	④	②	③	①	②	①	③	①	①

1 on a playing field / covered by a roof / watch two sports teams

2 did poorly in math / learns from his mistakes / a famous saying

3 keeping in touch with / three months ago / on the park bench

4 open a clinic / be wealthy / in a rich country

5 pick me up / I'll walk home / Come home right

6 lots of smoke / Where exactly / it's on fire / let the police know

7 very chilly / a carrot nose / Let's build a friend / and a muffler

8 under my bed / it had six arms / Ugly / you imagined something horrible

9 right over there / our science project

10 a smaller size / bring you a 95 / need to try on

11 Mary is not younger / not as old as / the heaviest

12 very nice of you / I'm glad / we have met before / another watch

13 that much money / a credit card / aren't very safe / lend you the rest

14 check out / Certainly / I stayed two nights / look it over

15 saw the doctor / too sick to study

16 my gate green / paint on your hands / I can't get it off / should wear gloves

17 a pair of shoes / romance film / the charges for using / the wrong building

18 for your effort / I can't believe it / the best scores

19 First of all / make a reservation / For how many people

20 it's been a long time / in the playground / this summer

1	2	3	4	5	6	7	8	9	10
③	②	③	①	②	②	④	②	②	①
11	12	13	14	15	16	17	18	19	20
③	②	①	③	②	③	②	③	①	④

1 on the blackboard / a student's notebook / raising her hand

2 of heavy snow / the temperature is getting colder / Trucks are clearing the roads

3 a history quiz / my finger still hurts / in a car door / give it back soon

4 No, I couldn't / I was playing soccer / did your team win / a great match

5 for three hours / and a temple / see the statue

6 A journalist / fiction stories / I make up

7 Just do your best / I said hello / It's over there / in the newspaper

8 be a little late / in about 20 minutes / No problem

9 A person's personality / how they look / than appearance

10 on the school yard / packages of snacks / throw away their trash

11 Is it straight / got a perm / Long curly hair

12 once a month / join the club / you must speak English / come and improve

13 She is a waitress / gives them a menu / to the table

14 any other age group / volunteer for fewer hours / The least number of

15 this semester / the final exams finish / three days after that / after the last day

16 I can't go out / play computer games tonight / a good way to make

17 Walk for two blocks / It's on the corner / and turn right / that's right

18 a lot of noise / with each other / stop talking / leave the classroom

19 to the amusement park / a good idea / It's a holiday / lots of rides

20 returning from the army / the military camp / too long ago / finished his duty

1	2	3	4	5	6	7	8	9	10
④	②	①	④	④	③	②	②	③	②
11	12	13	14	15	16	17	18	19	20
①	②	②	③	④	③	②	③	①	②

1 Luckily he wasn't hurt badly / on a red light / when walking and biking

2 the school's writing contest / in my classroom / Here it is / next period

3 are being very noisy / tell them not to make

4 I'm afraid / a yearly checkup / they make sure / a valuable tool

5 Thanks for inviting me / between 5th and 6th / across from a park

6 I couldn't type / spill something on it / The mouse is fine / a new keyboard

7 For what day / any seats available / at what time / that is possible

8 June 10th / on this Thursday / On the 13th / if you haven't

9 Is that all / got my allowance / go see a movie / Did you have fun

10 meet him again / he suggested / won first prize / Which ones / Where were you

11 the second Saturday / go all weekend / as long as possible / No, I can't

12 Where are newspapers located / chewing gum / 40 cents a package / two dollar bill

13 that's too long / Let's just leave / We can't do that

14 His plane will be / look there / behind schedule

15 go on the show / be a contestant / how to apply

16 Why so early / any plans / Which would you prefer / modern version

17 Weren't you hurt / I've just withdrawn money / look like / pictures of criminals

18 You can't see / to copy it / did the right questions

19 on my bill / not four nights / a snow storm / It's our mistake

20 I'd love to / have a party / you have a good time / I can't go

A

1. regular 보통의, 정기적인
2. annual 1년의, 연간의
3. musical instrument 악기
4. borrow 빌리다
5. remind (~에게 ...을) 생각나게 하다, 상기시키다
6. government 정부
7. overtake 추월하다
8. environment 환경, 주위
9. pollution 오염, 공해
10. cough 기침(하다)
11. community 공동체, 지역사회
12. volunteer 지원하다, 자원봉사하다
13. prefer 더 좋아하다, 선호하다
14. grade 점수, 성적
15. astronaut 우주비행사
16. repairperson 수리공, 수리인, 수리업자
17. include 포함하다
18. bother 괴롭히다, 성가시게 하다
19. comfortable 편안한
20. available 이용할 수 있는

B

1. d	2. e	3. j
4. o	5. h	6. m
7. a	8. b	9. g
10. k	11. c	12. i
13. n	14. f	15. l

C

1. a. give	2. b. to	3. b. used to
4. c. for	5. b. watching	6. a. to close

D

1. have	2. out of	3. for
4. either	5. was	

A

1. watch out 조심하다, 주의하다
2. luggage 수화물, 소형 여행가방
3. cause ~의 원인이 되다, 일으키다, 초래하다
4. activity 활동
5. harmful 해로운, 위험한
6. console 위로하다, 위문하다
7. electricity 전기
8. waste 낭비하다, 허비하다
9. involve ~을 수반하다, ~와 관련이 있다
10. emergency 비상사태
11. temperature 온도
12. chase 뒤쫓다, 추격하다
13. fall down 넘어지다, 쓰러지다
14. crop 농작물, 수확물
15. grateful 고마운, 감사하는
16. vegetable 야채, 채소
17. height 키, 신장, 높이
18. healthy 건강한, 건강에 좋은
19. pharmacy 약국
20. salmon 연어

B

1. j	2. i	3. g
4. n	5. f	6. l
7. b	8. a	9. c
10. e	11. o	12. h
13. k	14. d	15. m

C

1. c. telling	2. b. among	3. a. due
4. a. at	5. b. sounds like	
6. b. the other hand		

D

1. Put	2. Hold	3. off
4. most	5. cost	

WORD AND EXPRESSION REVIEW • TEST 5-6

A

1. develop 현상하다
2. director (영화)감독
3. bother 괴롭히다, 귀찮게 하다, 폐를 끼치다
4. avoid 피하다
5. exchange 환전하다, 교환하다
6. traffic 교통(량), 왕래, 통행
7. expire 만기가 되다, (기간이) 끝나다
8. validity 효력, 유효성
9. deposit 예금하다, 맡기다
10. carry 가지고 가다, 옮기다
11. vote 선출하다, 표결하다
12. medicine 약
13. passenger 승객, 여객
14. row 열, (좌석)줄
15. fasten 묶다, 조이다, 단단히 고정시키다
16. prepare 준비하다
17. destroy 파괴하다, 훼손하다
18. household 가족, 가구, 가정
19. consider ~라고 생각하다, 간주하다, 여기다
20. continent 대륙, 육지

B

1. l	2. i	3. b
4. o	5. g	6. h
7. m	8. f	9. k
10. k	11. n	12. a
13. d	14. j	15. e

C

1. c. out of	2. a. not go	3. c. make
4. b. by	5. a. much	6. b. well

D

1. treat	2. corner	3. it
4. stuck	5. on	

WORD AND EXPRESSION REVIEW • TEST 7-8

A

1. portable 휴대용의, 들고 다닐 수 있는
2. feed ~에게 먹이를 주다
3. cage (짐승의) 우리
4. allowance 용돈
5. reservation 예약
6. round trip 왕복여행, 왕복표
7. charge 요금, 비용
8. upset 뒤집힌, (위장이) 불편한
9. pleasure 기쁨
10. clerk 점원, 판매원
11. groceries 식료 잡화류
12. field trip 견학, 현장학습
13. improve 개선하다, 향상(발달)시키다
14. various 다양한
15. tend to ~하는 경향이 있다
16. sneeze 재채기하다
17. registered mail 등기 우편
18. cherish 소중하게 여기다
19. lend 빌려주다
20. hardworking 근면한, 열심히 일(공부)하는

B

1. j	2. l	3. e
4. b	5. i	6. h
7. a	8. k	9. n
10. m	11. o	12. c
13. d	14. g	15. f

C

1. c. of	2. b. hearing	3. a. not go
4. b. What	5. c. working	6. b. been

D

1. in	2. see	3. such
4. otherwise	5. sure	

A

1. nervous 불안한, 두려워하는
2. scared (of) 겁나는, 무서운
3. line-up 사람(물건)들의 열(줄)
4. latest 최신의
5. amazing 놀랄 정도의, 굉장한
6. in fashion 유행하고 있는
7. ripe 붉고 탐스러운, 잘 무르익은
8. prescription 처방전, 처방약
9. spell ~을 철자하다, 철자를 말하다
10. wheat 밀, 소맥
11. pharmacy 약국
12. personally 개인적으로
13. garbage 쓰레기
14. reduce 줄이다, 삭감하다
15. criminal 범인, 범죄자
16. decide to ~하기로 결정하다, 결심하다
17. device 장치
18. sore 아픈, 쑤신
19. by the way 그런데, 어쨌든
20. thief 도둑

B

1. c	2. k	3. h
4. g	5. l	6. d
7. o	8. j	9. f
10. n	11. e	12. i
13. b	14. a	15. m

C

| 1. b. to take | 2. c. take | 3. a. as |
| 4. c. see | 5. b. sounds like | 6. a. on |

D

| 1. look like | 2. at home | 3. in |
| 4. hear | 5. way | |

A

1. politely 공손히, 예의 바르게
2. considerate 사려 깊은
3. speed limit 제한 속도
4. government 정부
5. draw 그리다, 긋다
6. physical education 체육
7. greasy 기름진, 기름이 많은
8. appreciate 고맙게 생각하다, 감사하다
9. referee 심판
10. illegal 불법의, 반칙의
11. theater 극장
12. amusement park 놀이공원, 유원지
13. daily 매일의, 나날의
14. suggest 권하다, 제안하다
15. principal 교장, 회장, 사장, 우두머리
16. announce 알리다, 발표하다
17. forgive 용서하다
18. bow 머리를 숙이다, 절하다, 인사하다
19. behave 행동하다, 처신하다
20. allow 허락하다, 허가하다

B

1. e	2. l	3. k
4. o	5. m	6. g
7. b	8. n	9. a
10. d	11. f	12. j
13. i	14. c	15. h

C

| 1. a. do | 2. c. from | 3. c. hands |
| 4. a. ease | 5. c. make | 6. a. would |

D

| 1. used | 2. do I | 3. go |
| 4. keep | 5. how | |

WORD AND EXPRESSION REVIEW • TEST 13-14

A

1. opposite ~의 맞은편에
2. ancient 고대의
3. tray 쟁반, 요리를 담은 접시
4. pollute 더럽히다, 오염시키다
5. environment 환경, 주위
6. surgeon 외과의사
7. rush 서두르다, 급히 행하다
8. business management 경영학
9. look for ~을 찾다, 구하다
10. common 보통의, 평범한
11. facial 얼굴의
12. traffic jam 교통체증, 차량정체
13. appointment 약속, 예약
14. cancel 취소하다
15. creative 독창적인, 창의적인
16. pot 단지, 항아리, 냄비
17. explain 설명하다
18. apologize 사과하다
19. celebrate 축하하다, 거행하다
20. protect 보호하다, 지키다

B

1. c	2. f	3. h
4. m	5. d	6. o
7. l	8. n	9. b
10. e	11. i	12. k
13. j	14. a	15. g

C

1. a. but	2. c. from	3. b. caught
4. b. holding	5. a. in	6. c. to

D

1. say	2. wink	3. got
4. chance	5. for	

WORD AND EXPRESSION REVIEW • TEST 15-16

A

1. dish 접시, 식기
2. weigh 무게를 달다, 무게(체중)가 나가다
3. fitness center 헬스클럽
4. violence 폭력
5. educational 교육적인, 교육상의
6. poison 독, 독물
7. jewelry 보석류, 장신구류
8. bite 깨물다
9. frightened (of~) ~을 무서워하는
10. bark 짖다, 짖어대다
11. stranger 낯선 사람, 남
12. stuff 물건, 재료
13. chores 집안일, 허드렛일
14. literature 문학
15. analyst 분석가
16. insect 곤충, 벌레
17. concentrate 집중하다
18. device 장치, 기계
19. relatives 친척
20. satisfied 만족스러운, 만족하는

B

1. k	2. m	3. o
4. j	5. c	6. b
7. e	8. d	9. n
10. i	11. a	12. g
13. f	14. h	15. l

C

1. b. did I play	2. c. having	3. a. either
4. c. from	5. b. make	6. a. to

D

1. ride	2. wrong	3. difference
4. matter	5. out	

A

1. librarian 도서관원, 사서
2. repair shop 수리점, 수리공장
3. notice 통지, 알아차리다, 주의하다
4. parcel 소포, 꾸러미
5. errand 심부름, 용건, 볼일
6. avenue 대로, 큰 가로
7. rice cake 떡
8. palace 궁궐, 궁전
9. alone 혼자
10. evil 악, 악마
11. instead 대신
12. give up 포기하다, 단념하다
13. except ~을 제외하고, ~외에는
14. contact 접촉하다, 연락하다
15. wealthy 유복한, 풍족한
16. district 지구, 지역
17. chilly 추운, 차가운, 으스스한
18. wallet 지갑
19. effort 노력, 수고
20. location 위치

B

1. c	**2.** o	**3.** m
4. a	**5.** n	**6.** b
7. f	**8.** i	**9.** d
10. k	**11.** g	**12.** j
13. h	**14.** l	**15.** e

C

1. b. smoking	**2.** a. of	**3.** b. in touch
4. c. on	**5.** c. set	**6.** a. too

D

1. myself	**2.** no see	**3.** here
4. job	**5.** should	

A

1. raise 올리다, 들어올리다
2. attention 주의, 주목
3. severe 맹렬한, 심한
4. statue 상, 조각상
5. fiction 소설, 꾸민 이야기, 허구
6. personality 성격, 인격
7. appearance 외모, 외관
8. policy 정책, 방침
9. ability 능력
10. semester 학기
11. have fun 재미있게 놀다
12. period 기간, 수업시간
13. yearly 매년의, 연1회의
14. tool 도구, 방법
15. properly 올바르게, 알맞게, 적당히
16. bill 지폐, 청구서, 계산서
17. contestant 경기자, 대회 참가자
18. reserve 예약하다, 보유하다, 남겨두다
19. withdraw 돈을 인출하다
20. receptionist 접수계, 접수원

B

1. c	**2.** k	**3.** g
4. h	**5.** n	**6.** i
7. d	**8.** o	**9.** l
10. b	**11.** j	**12.** a
13. f	**14.** e	**15.** m

C

1. c. couple	**2.** a. make up	**3.** b. get on
4. b. so that	**5.** a. if	**6.** c. work

D

1. date	**2.** in	**3.** between
4. make	**5.** take	